The National Center
for Improving Science Education

The National Center for Improving Science Education (NCISE) is a division of The NETWORK, Inc., a nonprofit organization dedicated to educational reform. The center's mission is to promote change in state and local policies and practices in science curriculum, teaching, and assessment. We carry out our mission by providing a range of products and services to educational policy makers and practitioners who work to strengthen science teaching and learning all across the country.

Our products and services are oriented toward practical guidance for those who are responsible for the day-to-day decisions that shape diverse learning environments, preschool to postsecondary. We are dedicated to helping all stakeholders in science education reform, including the postsecondary institutions that train prospective science teachers, to promote better science education for all students.

NCISE
Advisory Board Members

The
Future of
Science
in Elementary
Schools

Senta A. Raizen
Arie M. Michelsohn
Editors

The Future of Science in Elementary Schools

Educating Prospective Teachers

 Jossey-Bass Publishers
San Francisco

Substantial discounts on bulk quantities of Jossey-Bass books are available to corporations, professional associations, and other organizations. For details and discount information, contact the special sales department at Jossey-Bass Inc., Publishers. (415) 433-1740; Fax (415) 433-0499.

For sales outside the United States, contact Maxwell Macmillan International Publishing Group, 866 Third Avenue, New York, New York 10022.

Manufactured in the United States of America. Nearly all Jossey-Bass books and jackets are printed on recycled paper containing at least 10 percent postconsumer waste, and many are printed with either soy- or vegetable-based ink, which emits fewer volatile organic compounds during the printing process than petroleum-based ink.

Library of Congress Cataloging-in-Publication Data

The future of science in elementary schools : educating prospective
  teachers / Senta A. Raizen, Arie M. Michelsohn, editors.
      p.   cm. — (The Jossey-Bass education series)
  Includes bibliographical references and index.
  ISBN 1-55542-624-7
  1. Science—Study and teaching (Elementary)—United States.
  2.   Science teachers—Training of—United States.   I. Raizen, Senta
A. II. Michelsohn, Arie M., date. III. Series.
LB1585.3.F88   1994
372.3′044—dc20   93-41154
                                                                         CIP

FIRST EDITION
HB Printing   10 9 8 7 6 5 4 3 2 1   *Code 9422*

The
Jossey-Bass
Education Series

Contents

Preface

A strong science education for all students is not a luxury but a necessity. Given the complexities of a society increasingly dependent on emerging technologies, understanding science has become vital for all individuals: to help them manage their personal lives, to become involved citizens, and to contribute to both the economy and their own welfare as skilled and intelligent workers. Science offers the opportunity for students to investigate problems logically and systematically and make informed decisions based on evidence. Through science, students can learn to have an inquiring mind that allows them to face change and uncertainty.

The study of science should begin in the earliest grades to cultivate and nourish the innate curiosity of children and develop within them analytical habits of mind they will be able to use throughout their lives. Elementary school science education lays the foundation for all later science education. A poor foundation will make successful science learning more difficult in the later grades; even worse, a poor early start will often lead to negative impressions of science and turn students away from any study of science later in their educations.

Although necessary, the acquisition of basic scientific facts and principles is insufficient for students to function successfully in the twenty-first century. Motivation for active student involvement in the science learning process should flow naturally from real-world contexts and problems that interest students. Young people need to learn how to ask probing questions, not passively accept superficial answers. They need to investigate deeply, not merely take perfunctory notice. They need to communicate, not regurgitate. They need to acquire a level of scientific literacy and critical thinking skills that will enable them to make informed decisions about the myriad science-related problems they will face as adults: weighing the benefits of various medical treatments, deciding on the safety of pesticides or food additives, or reconciling economic and ecological needs when voting on whether to preserve local wetlands or build a new highway through them.

Within the past decade, a clear consensus has emerged in science education: for science to engage young students and allow them to develop and hone their inquiry and reasoning abilities, the teaching of elementary school science will have to change radically. And such change will require major reforms in the preparation of elementary school teachers.

Recommendations for improving science education fill the reform documents of the 1980s. (The 1990s are characterized by the development of standards for what citizens of the twenty-first century should know and be able to do in science.) All the reports are quick to point out that making the new vision of science *learning* a reality requires a new vision of science *teaching*. The United States needs versatile teachers who are effective facilitators of investigation rather than didactic agents of authority, teachers who understand not only the sources of subject matter knowledge but also the intricate dynamics of the learning process, who have a lifelong commitment to enhance practice and create learning communities both within their own schools and throughout the nation.

While science teachers who possess these characteristics certainly do exist, science teaching in general remains embedded in the old tradition of lecturing from fact-filled textbooks. The problem is particularly acute in elementary schools, where science—if it is taught at all—often receives minimal attention in the curriculum. Many elementary school teachers do not feel well prepared to teach science (Weiss, 1987); they tend to leave it until the end of the day (Kidder, 1989) and use a textbook as their major resource (Weiss, 1987).

Over the next decade, some 250,000 elementary school teachers will be added to the current pool of 1.7 million (U.S. Department of Education, 1993a); by conservative estimates, another 400,000 new entrants will be needed as replacements for teachers who are retiring or leaving the profession for other reasons. We believe that the improvement of preservice teacher education in general, and of the science component of preservice programs in particular, are critical and fundamental levers for education reform that have been slighted in policy and reform action. Concentrating on preservice education can reduce the continual need for in-service retrofitting and remediation, which is more costly than educating teachers correctly in the first place.

Purpose of the Book

The Future of Science in Elementary Schools addresses the critical gap in science education reform. The focus of the book is on how the 650,000 new elementary school teachers who will be needed over the next decade can be educated to teach science effectively. We at the National Center for Improving Science Education undertook the writing of this book because we believe that science learning is important for all students, must start in the early grades, and can be improved only if the preparation in science of elementary school teachers is fundamentally reformed.

Audience

The book is aimed primarily at four groups: individuals who make education policy at the state level; administrators in colleges and universities, school districts, and schools; people responsible for developing, implementing, and administering preservice teacher education programs; and college and university instructors and school teachers responsible for instruction in science courses, science methods courses, and student teaching or other clinical experiences for prospective elementary school teachers. In our view, action is needed at all these levels.

We believe, however, that our recommendations regarding prospective elementary school teachers apply equally to K-6 science specialist teachers, but with additional preparation for the latter in science and science pedagogy relevant to the elementary grades. (In 1988, such specialist teachers made up about 1 percent of all elementary school teachers; most of the specialist teachers began their careers with majors in elementary education [Raizen and Britton, 1993].)

Organization and Content

The Future of Science in Elementary Schools is organized into eight chapters. The first three chapters provide background information by putting prospective elementary school teachers' education in science into the larger context of science teaching and learning and current reforms in science education and teacher education. Chapter One summarizes the status of science education as it is currently practiced in elementary schools. Chapter Two serves in part as an explanation for this status by providing profiles of teachers responsible for grades K–6 instruction—who they are and what kind of science education and experiences they have had. Chapter Three contrasts what preservice education has prepared elementary school teachers to do in the classroom today with what teachers at that level should know and be able to do in science, according to the general framework proposed by the National Board for Professional Teaching Standards.

The core of the book, Chapters Four through Seven, focuses on our vision of the education in science of prospective elementary school teachers. This vision is founded on the new research-based approach to science teaching and learning, which stresses the development of conceptual understanding through the construction of new knowledge in real-world contexts. This approach requires that teachers become facilitators of investigation, not individuals handing on knowledge conceived and developed by others. Teaching itself is seen as a creative process, a constant reinvention and adaptation of instructional strategies to motivate students and advance their learning. Teacher education must provide the foundation that will enable prospective teachers to develop into masters of curriculum interpretation who have a deep understanding of how students learn science.

Chapter Four develops a model for coordinating program

elements in the science portion of elementary school teacher education programs. Chapter Five presents approaches to the science subject matter to be included in programs for prospective elementary school teachers: what science content they should know and what they should know about the process of science. Chapter Six describes what prospective teachers should know about teaching science and what kinds of teaching experiences they should have before becoming provisionally qualified teachers. This chapter also provides information on current programs and practices in institutions that educate prospective elementary school teachers. Chapter Seven discusses some alternatives for structuring the preservice program. These alternatives are illustrated by means of various scenarios that indicate how the features identified as integral to a good program can be embedded in a variety of structures and settings.

In Chapter Eight, we make recommendations on how to bring about needed improvements. The recommendations deal with current impediments to change and suggest how various key institutions and people in them can implement the necessary reforms.

To provide further context for consideration of our recommendations, the book concludes with an appendix that summarizes a study of current practices in science education of prospective elementary school teachers conducted by the National Center for Improving Science Education (Michelsohn and Hawkins, 1993). The study served as part of the research on which *The Future of Science in Elementary Schools* is based.

Acknowledgments

We gratefully acknowledge the help given to us by many individuals who supplied materials and made suggestions for this book. While the list is too long to acknowledge each person individually, we wish to give special thanks to Paul Kuerbis, Colorado College, and William Ritz, California State University, Long Beach, for their review of the manuscript and their critical comments, which greatly helped to improve it. We also want to thank the members of the Advisory Board of the National Center for Improving Science Education (see list in the front of the book), who reviewed the manuscript and made valuable suggestions for improvement. In addition, we want to acknowledge Simon Hawkins, of the center, for his invaluable help in documenting pertinent research and the practices of institutions of higher education in preparing prospective elementary school teachers. Thanks are also due to Susan Callan for her supervision and careful attention in producing the many drafts of this book, to LaDonna Dickerson for her patient work in word processing, and to Sue Martin and our other colleagues at The NETWORK for their assistance in preparing the final manuscript.

Finally, we wish to express special thanks to the Andrew W. Mellon Foundation, the John D. and Catherine T. MacArthur Foundation, and the Pew Charitable Trusts, which, because of their commitment to the improvement of science education, funded the work of the panel and staff reflected in this book. Without their support, the book would not have been possible; however, its contents do not necessarily reflect the views of the sponsoring foundations.

Washington, D.C.   SENTA A. RAIZEN
November 1993   ARIE M. MICHELSOHN

The Editors

Senta A. Raizen is director of the National Center for Improving Science Education. She is the major author of several of the center's reports on science education in elementary, middle, and high school.

Raizen holds college and advanced degrees in chemistry and began her career as an industrial chemist; she is also certified as a high school chemistry teacher. She is a fellow of the American Association for the Advancement of Science and a member of the American Educational Research Association.

From 1980 to 1988, Raizen staffed several education activities for the National Academy of Sciences/National Research Council. She was study director for the NRC's Committee on Research in Mathematics, Science, and Technology Education and for the Committee on Indicators of Precollege Science and Mathematics Education. She was also responsible for the reports produced by these committees, including the most recent one, *Improving Indicators of the Quality of Science and Mathematics Education in Grades K-12.* From 1974 to 1978, Raizen was associate director of the National Institute of Education, in charge of programs to disseminate and apply research results to education. Prior to that she was a senior researcher at the RAND Corporation and, for ten years, a program official in science education at the National Science Foundation.

Raizen is the author of a number of papers and monographs on educational assessment, education policy, and science education, including an extensive review of research and policy relevant to reforming education for work. She worked with the Council of Chief State School Officers to develop a science framework for the 1994 science assessment to be conducted by the National Assessment of Educational Progress and with the International Association for the Evaluation of Educational Achievement to plan the Third International Mathematics and Science Study. Raizen is also a member of the International Steering Committee for this study and serves in an advisory capacity to several national and international education studies, including the National Assessment of Educational Progress and the National Goals Panel.

Arie M. Michelsohn is assistant professor of science education at the University of Maryland, Baltimore County. He earned his B.A. degree (1982) at Columbia University in biochemistry and both his M.A. degree (1985) in biology and his Ph.D. degree (1991) in molecular and cellular neurobiology at the California Institute of Technology. His graduate research focused on the genetic and environmental factors that determine cell type during nervous system development. He has coauthored several articles on this subject in professional scientific journals.

Michelsohn's current research interests are in the design of interactive multimedia instructional materials for both teacher education in science and science education in middle schools and high schools. Michelsohn has taught high school chemistry, physics, biology, and mathematics and served as curriculum director for the inaugural year of a residential summer science program for high school students at the California Institute of Technology.

Before joining the faculty at Maryland, Michelsohn served on the staff of the National Center for Improving Science Education, where he directed a study of actual practice in the preservice science education of elementary school teachers and coordinated the study of teacher education that served as part of the research for this book.

The Contributors

This book is the result of a collaboration between the National Center for Improving Science Education (NCISE) and a panel convened to address the improvement of the preservice science education of elementary school teachers. The panel members and editors conceived the material in the book and took responsibility for writing various sections. They should be considered as coauthors; only the length of the list of names prevents their appearance on the title page.

Study Panel Members

Deborah Ball, associate professor of education, College of Education, Michigan State University

Carl Berger, director of instructional technology systems, University of Michigan, Ann Arbor

C. Edward Buchwald, Lloyd McBride Professor of Environmental Study and chair, Department of Geology, Carleton College, Northfield, Minn.

Sally Crissman, associate director, NCISE

Susan Loucks-Horsley, senior researcher, NCISE

Georgea Mohlman-Langer, associate professor of education, Eastern Michigan University

Michael Padilla, professor and head, Department of Science Education, University of Georgia, Athens

The
Future of
Science
in Elementary
Schools

1

Improving Science Education:
A Continuing Challenge

In 1989, the governors of all fifty states and the president proclaimed six lofty national education goals (National Education Goals Panel, 1991, p. ix). Three of the goals address mathematics and science education:

- Goal Three: By the year 2000, American students will leave grades four, eight, and twelve having demonstrated competency in challenging subject matter including . . . science. . . .
- Goal Four: By the year 2000, U.S. students will be first in the world in science and mathematics achievement.
- Goal Five: By the year 2000, every adult American will be literate and will possess the knowledge and skills necessary to compete in a global economy and exercise the rights and responsibilities of citizenship.

Nevertheless, the predominant view and practice of science education in schools all over the country are at odds with these goals.

Current Problems

First, science continues to rank low in school instruction. For example, the 1990 National Assessment of Educational Progress

1

(NAEP) in science found that less than half (45 percent) of fourth-grade students were in schools in which science was a priority, while 95 percent were in schools in which reading was a priority (Jones and others, 1992). The NAEP data also show that only half the students in the fourth grade reported having science almost every day, while 28 percent indicated that they never had science or had it once a week or less. Few fourth-grade students spend much time on science homework; only 20 percent report spending one or more hours per week on this. Moreover, less time is spent on science instruction than on instruction in other subjects.

Second, the quality of science instruction also leaves much to be desired. Teachers rely heavily on textbooks, which account for 90 percent of instructional materials in use in grades four through six (Weiss, 1987). Instruction focuses on factual information that is disconnected from experience and concept development (Bybee and others, 1989). Few opportunities exist for exploration and discovery, for developing analytical skills, or for relating science to other disciplines to foster an integrated understanding of the world. As a result, many students receive a poor introduction to science in the early grades, a situation compounded in later grades when students elect not to take additional science courses. For a more complete picture of the discouraging state of elementary science education, see *Science and Technology Education for the Elementary Years: Frameworks for Curriculum and Instruction* (Bybee and others, 1989), *Assessment in Elementary School Science Education* (Raizen and others, 1989), and *Developing and Supporting Teachers for Elementary School Science Education* (Loucks-Horsley and others, 1989).

Science is a low priority and is taught poorly in elementary schools for several interrelated reasons:

- Reading and basic arithmetic skills dominate the curriculum.
- Teachers do not understand the potential for language and mathematics development through science.
- Teachers are poorly prepared in science and do not feel comfortable teaching it.
- Teachers believe that science consists of a body of facts and do not understand the nature of science as a way of knowing.
- Administrative support for science is largely absent at this level.

United States students do not perform well when compared to their counterparts in other countries. The most recent international data on the performance in science of elementary school students date back to 1986. At that time, at age ten (grades four and five), U.S. students ranked eighth among students of fifteen countries, while students from Japan, Korea, Finland, and Sweden ranked first through fourth, respectively (International Association for the Evaluation of Educational Achievement, 1988). More recently, data available on thirteen-year-olds (that is, students having completed their elementary education) reveal that U.S. students rank thirteenth among students of fifteen countries (Lapointe, Askew, and Mead, 1992). Perhaps as dismaying are the disparities in science achievement among student groups within the United States. The 1990 NAEP data (Jones and others, 1992) on fourth graders already give early indication of a performance gap between males and females: males perform slightly better in earth and space sciences. This performance gap increases for all the physical sciences as students move through school (Jones and others, 1992). The gap is considerably greater, however, between non-Asian minority and white students. This is true for all sciences and shows up at the fourth-grade level as a 30- to 40-point difference on a 500-point scale. The NAEP data also reveal considerable disparities between achievement scores of advantaged and disadvantaged students.

A Decade of Reform

Over the past decade, several significant steps have been taken at the national, state, and local levels to improve science education. These efforts have proceeded in two stages (Raizen, 1991). The first stage, motivated in large measure by concerns about economic competitiveness, has given rise to policies intended to strengthen the academic rigor of high school and increase exposure to the science curriculum. Typical are such measures as lengthening the school day or year, increasing the number of science courses required for high school graduation and university entrance, and changing teacher certification requirements. The second stage, in contrast, has begun to address more fundamental reforms concerned with curriculum and instruction, assessment, organization and teaching conditions in schools, and support and staff development for teachers.

The formulation of the national goals has accelerated national initiatives to improve elementary science education.

• One of the first of these initiatives was the National Science Foundation–funded Triad projects designed to bring together publishers, developers, and schools to develop and disseminate improved curricula. Seven programs were funded in elementary school science, some of which were intended as comprehensive K–6 programs: the *Life Lab Science Program,* developed by the University of California at Santa Cruz; *Science for Life and Living,* the technology and science/health program developed by the Biological Sciences Curriculum Study (BSCS); and *Insights,* focused specifically on students in urban systems (largely minority and largely poor) and developed by the Education Development Corporation. In addition, there are *Kids Network,* developed by the Technical Education Research Center (TERC), which links classrooms electronically for joint science work, and *Full Option Science System* (FOSS), developed by the Lawrence Hall of Science for use with existing curricula.

• Several projects are national in scope. The American Association for the Advancement of Science's (AAAS) *Project 2061* is a comprehensive, multimillion-dollar initiative designed to reformulate the infrastructures, curricula, and approaches to teaching science from kindergarten through grade twelve. The National Science Teachers Association's (NSTA) *Scope, Sequence and Coordination Project,* another national reform movement, focuses on science education for grades seven through twelve but is likely to have a great deal of influence on kindergarten through sixth-grade education because students will need to be prepared appropriately for the proposed curricular coordination in middle school and high school. A number of states and local districts are engaged with AAAS and NSTA in these reform efforts.

• The National Science Foundation (NSF) has funded Statewide Systemic Initiative grants to facilitate statewide coordination of the major components of science and mathematics education reform, including restructuring teaching, revising curricula, designing new assessments, and reeducating teachers. About half the states have received or will receive funding under this program. All states are supposed to develop K–12 or K–16 programs eventually; Massachusetts, Rhode Island, South Dakota, and California, among others, have already developed innovative programs at the elementary school level.

• The Eisenhower state and national mathematics and science education programs are administered through the U.S. Department of Education. The state program, which is focused entirely on teacher development, is the largest (nearly $250 million per year) single precollege mathematics and science program supported by any federal agency. It provides formula grants to state and local education agencies and competitive grants to institutions of higher education.

• The U.S. Department of Education has also funded the Eisenhower National Clearinghouse for Mathematics and Science Education, together with ten regional consortia, to help schools adopt improved mathematics and science curricula, materials, and assessment tools and to provide guidance on effective teaching and in-service professional development.

• The U.S. Department of Energy's laboratories and facilities operate programs that engage their scientists, mathematicians, and engineers in working with teachers, students, and school districts to improve precollege science and mathematics education.

• National standards for science education are being developed in the areas of curriculum, assessment, and teacher development by panels of distinguished educators and scientists under the auspices of the National Research Council of the National Academy of Sciences.

• The U.S. Department of Education has awarded grants to a half-dozen states to define what, when, and how to teach using the new standards. The states also are to develop model guidelines for teacher education and teacher certification.

• A potentially very significant initiative, that of the Federal Coordinating Council for Science, Engineering, and Technology (FCCSET), is coordinating the efforts of the U.S. Department of Education, the National Science Foundation, and other agencies to improve science education. The release of *Pathways to Excellence* (Federal Coordinating Council for Science, Engineering, and Technology, 1993) marked the articulation of a unified vision of science education reform that includes all educational levels and emphasizes standards, curriculum and instructional material design, and teacher and faculty development. The document also stresses the encouragement of underrepresented groups to pursue study in science and the public understanding of science. A key strategy is the dissemination of exemplary programs, materials, and effective reform initiatives.

More recently, the NSF-sponsored Conference on Critical Issues in Reforming Elementary Teacher Preparation in Mathematics and Science (see Gardner, Cochran, and Tobin, 1993) brought together national leaders in teacher education to identify and disseminate innovations in preservice elementary teacher preparation and to encourage the development of other innovations. Reforms have been spurred by state and local efforts as well. California has taken the lead in instituting statewide science education improvement, using its new science curriculum framework as the focus of reform. An increasing number of states are using their guidelines or frameworks for teaching science to align their testing programs and, in some cases, their textbook adoption criteria and teacher certification standards with their vision of the science curriculum. In a different vein, the state of Kentucky has recently instituted sweeping structural reforms in grades K–3. Some of the changes include five- to eight-year-old students working side by side without textbooks, helping each other solve problems in real-world contexts. Schools are beginning to be reinvented, from the ground up, through local initiatives mediated by such consortia as the Coalition of Essential Schools, the Accelerated Schools Program, and the Center for Educational Renewal and at the national level through partnerships between the federal government and the private sector.

All these projects stress a vision of learning grounded in new conceptions of pedagogy that stress thinking and solving problems in real-world contexts and the creation of schools as collaborative learning environments. While not all these reforms have a specific focus on science, there is growing recognition among reformers of the importance of science in the curriculum and the application of contemporary thinking about teaching and learning to the teaching of science.

Addressing reform in such a comprehensive way will take time. Considering the many structural and social problems that continue to plague the nation's schools and the few changes that have occurred over the past decade, it is obvious that substantive reform in education in general and science education in particular will require a cooperative effort of major proportions from a broad base of individuals and institutions working concurrently on all levels, from elementary school to university. Our goal in this book is to ensure that the science education of preservice elementary school teachers is seen as a critical component in the systemic approach necessary to make real and lasting change a classroom reality.

2

How Well Are Elementary Teachers Being Prepared in Science?

Understanding how teachers are presently prepared will help shed light on the condition of science education described in Chapter One. The vignette below illustrates the contrast between two different approaches toward teaching science and the vision needed to reform it.

Carla and Jeita sat on the playground watching their third-grade classes and talking about the unit on leaves that was coming up in the next week. This was Carla's third year of teaching third-grade science and Jeita's second. As they compared notes, it became evident that they were approaching the same unit of study in very different ways. If someone looked in their classrooms in a week or two, children or no children, they would look quite different.

"I follow the textbook," Jeita said. "That way I'm sure the kids are getting the main points they ought to get. Quite honestly, I don't know enough about science to be sure that what I'd tell them about leaves, or any other science topic for that matter, is correct or not. I think it's very important my children get a good, strong science background so they don't end up as insecure as I am about un-

derstanding science. I make sure they know the vocabulary really well. If they know all the parts of the plant and what they do, I'll be happy. I've set a secret goal for myself to have my students do better on the end-of-the-chapter tests each year."

"That's exactly how I was taught science in my school," Carla responded, "and I regret it to this day. I tried to memorize all those names and did well on the tests, and now I can't remember a single thing. Last week a group of kids began asking me all sorts of questions about leaves and trees. They had been picking up leaves from that tree over there; I think it's a maple. They wanted to know why leaves change color, how a tree knows when to start the color change or to drop the leaves, and why some kinds of leaves turn red and some brown and some lots of colors. They were so interested that I decided to begin right there: with the questions they already have about what's right on our playground."

"What will you do next?" Jeita asked. "You have a whole bunch of questions that neither you nor the children know the answers to. How's that going to help any of you?"

Carla continued, "I want them to learn that they can answer questions about nature and find out for themselves, even discover how much they already know. The books in the library are one source of information, but that only tells them that they have to depend on something other than their own ability to observe and investigate. Last year I got kids into groups and for each question they had, I begun by having them fill out a chart like this [she showed Jeita a sheet of paper]:

How and Why Leaves Change Color

What we know	What we think we know	What we want to find out	Why we care
_____	_____	_____	_____
_____	_____	_____	_____

"As they filled in the chart," Carla explained, "they discovered that together they really knew quite a lot, and some things they thought they were sure of they really didn't know after all. They also discovered that there were quite a few specific things they wanted to find out.

"Once I knew what my students already knew, I helped them choose items from the list of things they wanted to find out. Then the groups, with my help, planned a way to go about it. For instance, one group wanted to find out if the color changes in the leaves of the maple went in sequence. Did they change from green to red to brown or did some change from green to red and others from green to brown? This group decided the best way to answer that question was to carefully observe the tree and its leaves themselves. They found a low branch and tagged some leaves and kept track of them for two weeks. Another group noticed that the leaves under the tree were all green for a while, and then mostly green and some yellow, and then fewer greens and more yellows and some reds, and so forth. They picked up fifty leaves every other day for three weeks and counted and graphed the number of each color. When all the groups were sharing results, they discovered they had the same color change sequence as the group that had tagged the individual leaves."

"But what about the leaves being the part of the plant that takes in carbon dioxide and gives off oxygen so animals can live? It would be criminal if we had a leaf study and the kids didn't even know the term photosynthesis," *Jeita worried.*

"Believe it or not," Carla countered, "they did know the term photosynthesis *by the end of our unit. But they learned it as part of their study of color change. As they got involved in their own investigations, they found more and more questions they really wanted to know the answers to, and one of them was why are leaves colored anyway? In every group there was someone who 'knew' that plants make food and that the leaves have something to do with it, but they weren't quite sure what. One group learned that the color was needed so sunlight could help the leaves make food for the plants, but that the plants needed water and air, too.*

"Then we had a class discussion. I asked how water gets to the leaves, and one student answered that the roots take the water from the ground up to the leaves. Then I asked what would happen to the water in the winter. After a brief silence, while I waited for students to think, a second student suggested that when it got cold enough, the water would freeze and couldn't get up to the leaves. Finally, in response to a classmate's comment that there aren't any leaves on trees in the winter, another student said, 'Maybe that's why the trees drop their leaves. If the trees can't use them, maybe they get rid of them so they don't have to take care of them.'

"When students begin linking concepts and making connections, I feel that all the time I've spent planning activities and paying attention to the

way I present material in class, even disciplining my-
self to use 'wait time,' is going to pay off for these
kids in the long run."

What does Carla do that makes her an effective teacher of science? She has a vision of science in the elementary classroom that includes major reform elements, some of which are illustrated in the vignette (see, for example, *Getting Started in Science: A Blueprint for Elementary School Science Education,* National Center for Improving Science Education, 1989).

• Carla knows that science learning is cumulative. Therefore, she wants her students to have many different sorts of science experiences that, taken together, present a coherent program of science knowledge and science processes.

• Carla knows that there are many ways to create a need to know—demonstrations, puzzles, videos, experiments, projects, or even just an intriguing question or two. The choice of which procedures to use will depend on many factors. Effective science teachers weigh the contextual factors and consistently draw on resources that translate a curriculum into motivating situations and activities.

• Because hands-on science stimulates children's innate curiosity about nature and thus encourages them to persist in the study of science, Carla works to incorporate developmentally appropriate investigations into her lesson units, gradually developing abstract concepts by using concrete hands-on experiences.

• Carla realizes that not all topics lend themselves to a hands-on approach, however. Therefore, she knows that she must support other lessons through student reading and library research, lectures, and class discussion.

• Because Carla knows that not all children learn in the same way, she weighs many considerations about how to conduct her lessons, what students might already know, how their prior knowledge might be coordinated with their current learning, and what different instructional materials and hands-on activities might be appropriate.

• Because Carla also knows that simply telling the right answer to children does little to change their conceptions, she encourages students to put together what they already know (for example, about color changes in leaves), what they can learn from further systematic observation, and what "expert" sources have to say.

- Carla sees new communication technologies as opening new avenues for learning. Therefore, she hopes to use good simulation and modeling software and link her students to a communications network that will let them work with their peers in other classrooms and, if possible, with scientists addressing the same problem.

- Carla uses a variety of ways to assess what her students have learned: short quizzes, systematic observations of their project work and recording of individual progress, review of homework, and oral and written responses to open-ended questions that ask students to apply their knowledge in novel situations. Because she knows that students vary in their preferred mode of expression, Carla provides a variety of contexts for assessing her students' science knowledge and skills.

- Carla sees herself as the director of her classroom as well as someone who can influence the wider school community. She manages the classroom environment, the curriculum, and science materials to best facilitate student learning. She meets on a regular basis with the second- and fourth-grade teachers at her school to try to create sequences of science instruction that will build on each other through several grades. She knows she cannot do her best unless the principal is supportive and the system in which she works allows teachers adequate planning time and consultation with colleagues; she seeks to obtain these conditions in her school and in her district. She looks forward to collaborating with science and science education faculty at the nearby state university to plan a mentor program for prospective teachers, using her science classes for their induction.

Background and Characteristics of Elementary School Teachers

Why is the reality of most elementary school science teaching so different from Carla's vision and from what reformers are advocating (Bybee and others, 1989)? To understand the great gap between Carla's classroom and most others, one must know how teachers are presently educated and whether their education and background prepare them to teach science effectively to the diverse types of children who make up the current elementary school population.

Preparation in Science and Science Teaching

In almost all of the nation's elementary schools, classroom teachers are responsible for science instruction (U.S. Department of Education, 1992a). Data show that most of these teachers have had limited exposure to science as undergraduates and in their professional training. Only 34 percent of all elementary school teachers have met the National Science Teachers Association (1983) standards for elementary school teachers (National Science Board, 1989), which recommend one course each in biology, physics, and earth science (Weiss, 1987). (It should be noted that new NSTA standards were adopted in 1992; they call for preparation of prospective elementary school teachers in the biological, earth/space, environmental, and life and physical sciences through laboratory and field-oriented experiences. The new standards [National Science Teachers Association, 1992] recommend a minimum of twelve semester hours in science courses and three semester hours in elementary science education.) As a consequence of this poor preparation in science, teachers have limited confidence in their ability to handle science. Whereas 82 percent of elementary teachers consider themselves well qualified to teach reading, only 15 percent feel the same way about their ability to teach physical and earth science; the figure is only slightly higher (27 percent) for life science (Weiss, 1987). Confidence increases with good preparation. Michael R. Vitale and Nancy R. Romance (1992) found that preservice teachers who had been exposed to innovative earth science curricula demonstrated more knowledge of the subject and expressed a greater enjoyment of teaching science and confidence in their own knowledge than preservice teachers who had experienced a more traditional curriculum.

Arnold Arons (1983) has pointed out that, in their understanding of science, many elementary school teachers start out being not much different from the students they teach. Understanding science concepts takes time; one cannot assimilate the abstract concepts and modes of thought that characterize scientific thinking through quick memorization. The process is not helped by the kind of instruction that most elementary school teachers are likely to have had in their high school and college science courses. Typically, that instruction has employed didactic, lecture-based approaches based on conveying information from the "expert" to the "novice"—precisely the kind of teaching that current reform efforts strive to avoid. Most elementary teachers have never been exposed to effective, inquiry-based instruction; they have no models on which to draw for their own students. In addition, most have probably had limited opportunities to study and reflect on the various ways in which students learn science and how to design and adapt materials and strategies to accommodate different learning styles. Considering both the quantity and quality of instruction in science and science teaching that most elementary school teachers have had, it is not surprising that so few feel well qualified to teach science.

The problems of insufficient and inappropriate preparation are not remedied by continuing education. Data show that the least prepared teachers are the ones least likely to participate in continuing education. Fully half of all elementary school teachers took their last science course(s) more than ten years ago; fewer than 30 percent have taken college-level science courses within the past five years (Raizen and Britton, 1993). If teachers had a basic understanding of science and science teaching before they assumed full-time classroom responsibilities, then in-service and staff development programs could carry them beyond the basics, serving to stimulate discussions of new research, new ideas, and new instructional approaches and materials. Unfortunately, at present, in-service programs are a quick but insufficient remedy for the missed opportunities of preservice education.

Composition of the Teaching Pool

A quite different problem is that the demographic composition of the elementary school teaching pool is mismatched to that of the student body (Kirby and Hudson, 1993). Ninety percent of all elementary school teachers are female (U.S. Department of Education, 1992b), 88 percent are white, 6 percent are black, and 6 percent are other races (U.S. Department of Education, 1992c). In contrast, the student body is more than 25 percent black and Hispanic (U.S. Department of Education, 1988), with that percentage on the increase.

A predominance of white female teachers presents several problems. As noted, in part because of teacher background and attitude, science instruction is often given short shrift in elementary schools. This inadequacy becomes more problematic for girls and minorities, who because of social biases, class differences, and/or societal pressure may be less interested in or prepared to learn science than are white males. Moreover, Jeannie Oakes (1990) suggests that girls and minorities have fewer opportunities than do boys and white children to participate in science-related activities outside of school. These factors prompt a vicious cycle, with those who are most likely to teach elementary school—women—receiving an inadequate science education, increasing the likelihood that they will teach science poorly and inadvertently promote the stereotype that females do not like or succeed in science. A similar cycle steers women and non-Asian minorities away from science as a profession. Thus, teachers who themselves have experienced little success in science may, through their practices, behaviors and attitudes, cull out youngsters who might be interested in and could achieve high standards in science. Even worse, because of societal messages, low achievement, and/or poor self-esteem not counteracted by the school or their teachers, students may eliminate themselves. As a result, women and non-Asian minorities remain underrepresented in science and in science teaching.

Having a majority of white teachers limits the opportunity that minority youngsters have of seeing people of their race or ethnicity in teaching roles, including that of teaching science (Ford and Varney, 1989; Pearson, 1985). This in turn may reduce the chance of minority children pursuing careers in prestigious academic fields, including science. The problems are exacerbated by the fact that many school teachers have not been trained to work successfully with students of different racial or ethnic groups or those who do not yet speak English well (Clewell, Anderson, and Thorpe, 1992). A lack of appreciation for the value of differences in the classroom can handicap the academic progress of children who are not part of the cultural mainstream.

But the demographic imbalance in teaching staff does not affect only minority students. Children's experiences in school exist in the context of their larger world, which tends to show white males as scientists and as those who make decisions involving science. The predominance of white teachers constricts opportunities for white students to see adults of ethnic and racial minority groups as teachers and as competent in science, which might help break down their stereotypes and misconceptions about people of color.

Schools appear to perpetuate the cycle in which students' exposure to poor or insufficient instruction in science in the early grades affects their career choices and job performance as adults, whether as teachers of science or in other science-related fields. And apparently, colleges do little to alter the traditional patterns.

Preservice Teacher Education

Nearly all elementary school teachers have gone through a teacher preparation program (Raizen and Britton, 1993), but the programs are varied and only about 40 percent meet the standards of the National Council for Accreditation of Teacher Education (1993). An overview of current practice in teacher education is useful in understanding why so few elementary school teachers are willing and able to teach science in the way that Carla does. Moreover, because science makes up a relatively small fraction of the preservice teacher preparation experience, it is important to view the science preparation of teachers within the broader context of the programs as a whole.

Institutions and Programs

Currently, nearly 1,200 postsecondary institutions in the United States produce elementary school teachers. In 1990, these institutions granted 48,623 bachelor's degrees in elementary education, or 52 percent of all bachelor's degrees in education. Roughly two-thirds (750) of the institutions are responsible for 90 percent of the education degrees. Thus, prospective elementary school teachers are educated in a great variety of institutions, although there is some concentration in the larger state colleges and universities traditionally oriented toward teacher education.

Not all newly qualified teachers go into teaching immediately. In 1991, 76 percent of all newly qualified teachers with bachelor's degrees applied for an elementary or secondary teaching job immediately before or just after receiving their degrees. Of those who applied, 71 percent were employed as regular or substitute teachers one year after graduation (U.S. Department of Education, 1993b).

Generally, teacher education programs operate at the undergraduate level. In the current teaching force, 53 percent of elementary school teachers hold a bachelor's degree as their terminal degree, usually with a major in education (National Education Association, 1992). In work related to this book and conducted by the National Center for Improving Science Education, Arie Michelsohn and Simon Hawkins (forthcoming) gathered information on the current state of teacher education programs. They conducted telephone interviews with individuals knowledgeable about the science aspects of most of the one hundred largest teacher-certifying programs throughout the country, as well as teacher education programs that had been nominated (by others, themselves, or through identification in the literature) as having implemented innovations in their programs. A total of 142 institutions were surveyed, and some site visits were conducted as well.

Michelsohn and Hawkins found that education majors typically fulfill a series of general education requirements, usually followed by a number of professional education courses that can be taken in almost any order. Comments from individuals interviewed indicate that, in some programs and some states, nearly half of the elementary certification candidates take their mathematics and science content courses at community colleges. (See Appendix at the back of this book for an overview of the study.) The education courses in the teacher education programs largely consist of methods courses, both general and subject area specific, and several other courses in such areas as educational psychology and the social context of education. Following these courses, education majors typically engage in up to a semester's worth of "student teaching," during which they assume increasing responsibilities in the classroom (Blank and Dalkilic, 1992).

Most elementary school teachers with a degree beyond the baccalaureate have a master's degree in education, reflecting either a decision made after college to enter the teaching profession (in which case the master's is their first professional teaching degree acquired after an initial liberal arts degree) or a career decision to pursue advanced professional certification in addition to an undergraduate degree in education. The acquisition of an advanced degree is rewarded in many districts with higher pay. In general, master's degree programs in elementary education are similar to the professional component of undergraduate education programs with respect to the content and sequence of courses required for professional training.

Problems and Issues

Those outside the immediate teacher education community have long questioned the quality of teacher preparation programs. According to a study by John Goodlad (1990), teacher education programs in general are plagued by three negative factors:

- Lack of focus and coherence of mission
- Lack of autonomy because of state mandates for certification that are based on course requirements rather than on program outcomes
- Lack of status of education programs and faculties within universities and in the opinion of the general public

Lack of focus and coherence manifests itself through a general failure to specify the overarching themes and goals of a program or identify critical curricular content. A general lack of coordination among the various components of the program exacerbates the problem. Most teacher education programs do not relate content to pedagogy except in the narrow sense of providing prospective teachers with a knowledge of subject matter activities that they will be able to use with their students. Few explicit connections are made between the theory studied in university-based course work in subject matter content (say, biology) and the classroom-based experiences in elementary grades (say, growing seeds) that make up student teaching. In fact, many supervisors of student teachers are hired as part-time faculty who do not participate in the conceptualization and oversight of the teacher preparation program as a whole or have the opportunity to communicate frequently with other faculty (Clifford and Guthrie, 1988).

The lack of autonomy and the detailed state mandates reflect an intrinsic ambivalence in the United States about whether teaching is a profession. For virtually all other professions, the authority for prescribing the course of study for qualifying for a particular profession is vested in the profession's practitioners; this is not the case for teaching. By and large, state legislatures either mandate how many of which kinds of courses teachers must take in order to be certified, or they do so indirectly by mandating the courses that teacher education programs must offer in order to be accredited. Although these procedures have recently been undergoing some change, they were generally still in place in the early 1990s. Some believe this lack of autonomy reflects a societal view toward women. A "feminized" profession such as teaching could hardly be worthy of self-governance, according to this view (Tyson, 1994; Hoffman, 1981).

The lack of status perhaps has had the greatest impact on teacher education policy. It stems in part from a long-standing opinion, expressed both within and outside the educational community, that teacher education courses lack substance and bear little relationship to the needs of future practitioners. Some critics have gone so far as to say that such courses exist only because of state mandates lobbied for by teachers' unions desiring a secure gate to the profession. These views have been current for a long time. The descriptions given by James B. Conant (1963) in his scathing report on teacher education programs in many ways resemble much more recent critiques (Goodlad, 1990, 1991; Carnegie Forum on Education and the Economy, 1986). For example, Goodlad (1990, pp. 262–263) writes of the requirements for general education courses: "One of the most glaring weaknesses throughout stemmed from the com-

mon assumption that undergraduate general-education requirements provide sufficient background for future teachers. This is a
dangerous assumption. A task of great magnitude—that of determining the education required to ensure that teachers will be capable of participating broadly in human discourse and that they
will be intellectual role models for their students—is scarcely being
addressed."

Negative opinions about education courses are not always
supported by evidence. The American Association of Colleges for
Teacher Education (1989) did, in fact, ask both teacher education
students and their instructors about the substance, rigor, and utility
of methods courses. The association found that most prospective
teachers and teacher educators consider teacher education courses to
be at least as rigorous as—and often more rigorous than—their
liberal arts courses. Validating the merit of at least some methods
courses, Harriett Tyson (1994) documents several visits to education
classes in her profiles of teacher education programs. She observed
that these classes were filled with intellectual discourse and a real
struggle on the part of students to grapple with substantive educational issues.

Negative opinions have been sufficiently pervasive, however,
to have had a significant effect on policy. A notable example is the
adoption of policies by a growing number of states that require prospective elementary school teachers to major in a content field rather
than in education. In 1991, six states required students to major in
a field other than education (Mastain, 1991), and at least two other
states, Virginia and Maryland, were discussing the adoption of a similar requirement. (By contrast, in 1991, thirteen states required students to major in education.) By requiring students to major in a
content area outside of education, states are ensuring that students
will take more hours of liberal arts courses. This policy stems in large
measure from recommendations of the Carnegie Forum on Education
and the Economy (1986) and the Holmes Group (1986), which envis-
age a four-year liberal arts program followed by a master's degree
program focused specifically on teacher preparation.

Some policy makers and leaders outside the education community have urged ridding the system of preservice education programs altogether, a position based on very little study or data. As

an alternative, they advocate strengthening liberal arts programs and instituting clinical teaching apprenticeships outside the auspices of teacher education institutions.

Despite these trends, teacher education programs still largely follow the traditional four-year program. In a survey of 407 universities with graduate education programs, Mei Jiun Wong and Russell T. Osguthorpe (1993) found that 55 percent offered only a four-year program for elementary teacher certification; the rest offered a four-year program along with other options. Wong and Osguthorpe point out that, even in those universities that offer more than one path for teacher certification, the four-year program tends to be the primary one. Obviously, the percentage of institutions offering only four-year certification programs would be much larger if one were to include institutions that do not have graduate education programs.

Science Content and Methods in Preservice Programs

Lack of coordination within preservice programs is particularly apparent in the science content and science methods components. A study by Kenneth R. Mechling, Carlton H. Stedman, and Kathleen M. Donnelan (1982) indicates that 82 percent of the forty-five leading teacher education institutions surveyed did not require specific courses in science content, leaving the selection to the students. About half of these forty-five institutions required only eight or fewer semester hours of science content of prospective elementary school teachers, practically the same numbers of hours required of *all* students, whether they expected to teach or not. Moreover, most of the science content courses taken by prospective elementary school teachers are the same as the undergraduate introductory science courses for all students (Mechling, Stedman, and Donnelan, 1982; Michelsohn and Hawkins, 1993), courses that have been criticized by such reports as *The Liberal Art of Science* (American Association for the Advancement of Science, 1990). In most of these courses, prospective elementary school teachers are presented with science as a body of factual knowledge taught didactically rather than in a spirit of inquiry—an approach that they perpetuate in their own school teaching. In fact, it could be argued that the reforms we recommend for future teachers apply equally to all non-science majors, who also need high-quality science experiences.

The Mechling, Stedman, and Donnelan (1982) study found that most teacher education programs also required prospective teachers to complete a three-semester-hour science methods course. Michelsohn and Hawkins (1993) have confirmed this in their study conducted some ten years later. Furthermore, their information indicates that in the majority of cases the science methods course is not coordinated with other aspects of the program. There is, for example, no emphasis on science in the student teaching experience that can build on what is learned in the science methods course. By and large, student teaching involves indoctrination into the mainstream elementary school curriculum, which—as noted earlier—contains little science, especially in the early grades. The substance of typical science methods courses usually involves the planning, performance, and microteaching of elementary school science activities that prospective teachers will be able to import directly into the classroom. Methods instructors indicate that one of their primary course objectives is to teach science process skills and in so doing overcome the fear that many teacher education students have about teaching science. Thus, methods courses tend to have a distinctly practical orientation. The limit of three credit hours makes it difficult to accomplish other objectives, such as compensating for poor content knowledge or pursuing concepts of effective science teaching. It appears that students planning to become teachers must often struggle on their own with the science content while at the same time trying to grapple with issues of how elementary school students learn science.

While the majority of teacher education institutions do require students to take some science courses and nearly all institutions require students to complete a science methods course, only twenty-six states have any science content requirement for elementary school teachers, and only twenty-nine states require them to complete course work in both science methods and mathematics methods (Blank and Dalkilic, 1992). It should be noted, however, that thirteen other states, while not laying out specific content requirements, do set general accreditation standards for teacher education programs, many of which require an unspecified amount of science (Mastain, 1991).

Among the states mandating science content courses, the range of requirements is from two to twelve semester hours; the average requirement is for six semester hours. There is still a considerable gap between the number and types of courses recommended by the NSTA and these mandates by the states (Blank and Dalkilic, 1992). Even so, as Betty J. Young and Theodore Kellogg (1993) point out, simply raising the number of credit hours required in science will not produce great changes unless course quality is improved as well. Both quantity and quality are lacking in the science content and science education components of preservice programs for prospective elementary school teachers. Furthermore, there may be a tendency for science methods instructors themselves to have less than exemplary backgrounds in science education. Lloyd Barrow (1987) characterizes the elementary science faculty he surveyed as "generalists rather than science education specialists (p. 562)." Nearly 39 percent of his respondents had had eighteen or fewer hours of science courses beyond the bachelor's degree, and 35 percent had had nine or fewer hours of science education courses beyond the bachelor's degree. In a study of the thirty-five graduate schools with the most science education faculty members, Robert E. Yager and Eric Zehr (1985) found that nearly 18 percent of the science education faculty had terminal degrees in general education.

Changes Under Way

Teachers not trained to match teaching strategies to students, context, and topic and with limited teaching repertoires are likely to have some difficulty teaching in the new school environments that reformers are advocating. Hence, most reform efforts include provisions for teacher development and enhancement, especially in science and mathematics. In-service programs to improve the science content knowledge of elementary school teachers and to acquaint them with inquiry-based approaches to teaching science have become a major funding priority in federal programs. The National Science Foundation invested $83 million in in-service programs in fiscal 1992, about 60 percent of which focused on elementary school teachers. (Interestingly, only $14 million was spent on all preservice programs.) The NSF plans to continue funding at this level through 1993 and 1994. It has also invested $39 million in the Curriculum/Materials Development program, which focuses on introductory college-level science, engineering, and mathematics courses. The program's aim is to make these courses more attractive to both science and nonscience majors, and especially future K–12 teachers (Federal Coordinating Council for Science, Engineering, and Technology, 1991). In addition, the NSF has initiated a new program of collaboratives involving industry and community agencies as well as schools and colleges to develop alternative approaches to science and mathematics education for teachers.

The FCCSET has set teacher in-service programs in science and mathematics as a high priority and plans to encourage member agencies to fund teacher institutes in science and mathematics for 600,000 teachers (particularly those at the elementary level) over the next five years (Federal Coordinating Council for Science, Engineering, and Technology, 1993).

More comprehensive national efforts to set rigorous standards for the teaching profession and for the institutions that prepare future teachers are currently under way. In 1991–92, Congress appropriated nearly $10 million to support the National Board for Professional Teaching Standards (NBPTS) in designing and implementing new, rigorous—though voluntary—licensing standards for experienced teachers (National Board for Professional Teaching Standards, 1992). First proposed in the Carnegie Forum on Education and the Economy (1986) report *A Nation Prepared,* the NBPTS is to provide a credentialing process for an upper tier of the teaching profession consisting of highly skilled teachers who have met rigorous professional standards. The standards set for this upper echelon of experienced teachers are expected to influence the standards set for the training of new teachers as well.

In tandem with the creation of the NBPTS has come a renewed effort on the part of the National Council for Accreditation of Teacher Education (NCATE) to raise accreditation standards for teacher education institutions, including standards in the science component of preservice programs for elementary school teachers. With minor modifications, the NCATE has adopted the NSTA science standards. The newest version of these standards (National Science Teachers Association, 1992) stresses the integration of science with other subject areas and the teaching of science using inquiry-based approaches and field experiences.

Considerable improvement efforts have been initiated by consortia of teacher education institutions, such as the Holmes Group, the Renaissance Group, (Goodlad, 1991), the Project 30 institutions (Project 30 Alliance, 1991), and the recently formed Salish group (consisting of twenty-six institutions, including Florida State University, Kansas State University, Michigan State University, Texas A&M, University of Georgia, University of Iowa, University of North Carolina, University of South Florida, and University of Texas). Also, the FCCSET has set as a priority the creation of eight regional consortia for teacher preparation, although none of the details of how they will be organized or operate have yet been formulated. The purpose of each of these consortia is to improve the teacher education programs of its constituent members. Out of these efforts have come innovations that link universities more closely with schools to form partnerships for teacher preparation, as well as attempts to foster increased collaboration between education faculty and liberal arts faculty. In the context of restructuring their programs as a whole, many of the institutions participating in these efforts have been grappling with alternative means of improving the science component of their elementary school teacher preparation program.

One of the unsettled issues in these reform efforts is whether to concentrate on a liberal arts, discipline-specific major in the undergraduate years followed by a year of graduate study concentrating on professional teacher preparation or to interweave subject matter learning with professional teacher education during the four undergraduate years. An argument for the first approach is to encourage prospective teachers to engage in depth with intellectually challenging subject matter in at least one discipline; an argument against it is the opportunity cost to the prospective teacher in terms of the costs of an additional year of schooling and a year of foregone income. No matter what the structure of preservice education, however, there is consensus that all prospective teachers need more subject matter education. Yet subject matter education should not be pursued to the exclusion of pedagogical education. Content courses need to be balanced by well-designed education courses that teach prospective teachers how to teach various subjects and provide opportunities for more contact with students of the age they are preparing to teach even before their formal practice teaching experience.

Challenges to Reform

This book addresses the challenge of reformulating teacher education programs in science so that Carla's vision of science in the elementary classroom can become a reality in most schools. However, a number of other obstacles to science education reform must be overcome as well. We note these briefly in order to set our discussion and recommendations on preservice teacher education in the context of the broader effort needed to reform science education in the elementary school.

First, the view of science as an ad hoc addition to an already crowded elementary curriculum must be changed in both the schools and the teacher education programs. Science holds great promise as a vehicle for curricular integration and as a context for teaching analytical thinking, communication skills, and mathematical skills. Considerable work remains to be done, however, to integrate science into the core elementary school curriculum in such a way that it becomes a primary source of instruction.

Second, instructional materials need to provide all students—university as well as elementary—with opportunities appropriate to their level to grapple with scientific concepts in some depth rather than require students to passively assimilate factual information. Moreover, students should be encouraged to demonstrate their learning achievements through such performance-based work as student portfolios, sustained projects, presentations of science investigations, and real-world problem solving (Raizen and others, 1989). While these are good prescriptions, translating them into practical classroom resources and practices is a formidable task. Indeed, recent research indicates that many new elementary school science texts claim to stress higher-order thinking in the questions they pose to students but in reality do not (Risner, Skeel, and

Nicholson, 1992). Teachers must have available to them new instructional materials and ways of assessing their students' learning that are truly consistent with contemporary goals for science education.

Although the past decade has produced a considerable amount of research on how students learn science and on performance-based assessments, new curricula, instructional materials, and assessments based on tested pedagogical theory consonant with this research are scarce. Recent experience in Vermont (Koretz and others, 1992) and research on performance-based assessment (Shavelson and others, 1991) indicate that there are still significant problems with the new approaches to assessment, such as their reliability and the difficulty in developing scoring systems. Educators need to continue to work on ways to implement constructivist and performance-based approaches to curriculum, instruction, and assessment in the classroom.

Third, and most salient to this book, the distinction between traditional, didactic school science curricula and new curricula that stress active student engagement in science crucially affects what teachers need to know and be able to do. Whereas basic knowledge of science content and classroom management skills may have sufficed for efficient didactic teaching, reform science curricula require that teachers act as facilitators of students' hands-on investigations, as well as investigations using written and oral sources of expertise. Teachers must know how and be prepared to shift focus in response to or in anticipation of a myriad of circumstances both inside and outside the classroom. For the teacher-as-facilitator model to become institutionalized as practice, the shift from didactic teaching to facilitative teaching needs to be accompanied by a shift in teacher education strategies. Preservice programs must focus on the development of the advanced knowledge and skills needed to exercise complex pedagogical judgments. Development of expertise in such judgments requires more than science content knowledge and acquaintance with inquiry-based science activities, though these are necessary components. Developing pedagogical judgment requires consistent, long-term teacher development strategies, beginning in the earliest phases of a teacher's education.

Because of their changed role, teachers should be the ones leading the way to overcoming these challenges. They must create a demand for instructional materials that are consistent with what they know to be the most effective approaches to teaching science, and they should participate in the development and evaluation of such materials. Moreover, teachers should be core collaborators in expanding the research on what instructional strategies work best with particular groups of students and how to assess the efficacy of these strategies. They should be principal contributors to a professional literature that documents this clinical research and should discuss this literature on a regular basis in professional meetings and conferences. In essence, teaching is, in our view, a much more complex and dynamic process than more traditional views may admit.

3

The Qualities
of an Effective
Teacher of Science

Carla, one of the teachers depicted in Chapter Two, has the special combination of knowledge, skills, and disposition needed to create a classroom environment that fosters a deep understanding of science concepts and processes. It is the function of the teacher education program to help prospective teachers develop such abilities. In this chapter, we elaborate further on what elementary teachers need to know and be able to do in order to support their students' science learning, thus providing a basis for our discussion of optimal teacher education activities and structures in later chapters.

For this book on preservice teacher education, we considered discussing what the "graduating" teacher education student (that is, the newly certified teacher) should know and be able to do. This picture of an emerging professional was, in fact, impossible to create, for it required working backward from a depiction of the experienced professional teacher, qualifying that image as "beginning to", "usually", and "needs to acquire through practice." We realized that newly certified teachers must have a base of knowledge and skills that will allow them to build continually toward the excellence of exemplary teachers but that they will need both practice and continuing education to use their knowledge and skills as consistently, thoughtfully, selectively, and sensitively as do experienced teachers. We agree with Christopher M. Clark (1984, p. 5), who describes newly qualified teachers as "well-started novices" rather than "inexperienced experts." Clark describes these novices as having "a general orientation of the profession, some as yet unpracticed pedagogical skills, and some academic skills. . . . [T]he acknowledged role of the novice is to learn, to actively continue in . . . development toward expert status." Because this is the ultimate goal, we decided to depict the knowledge and skills of the professional, experienced teacher—admittedly an ideal one—acknowledging that the preservice program is but the beginning of the development of the professional, who will continue to grow over the entire teaching career.

We have resisted the temptation to create a complete list of our own of what teachers need to know and be able to do. Instead, we have chosen to take the recommendations made by the National Board for Professional Teaching Standards (1991), which we heartily endorse, and both elaborate on and adapt them for elementary science teaching. The NBPTS describes professional teachers as follows:

- Teachers are committed to students and their learning.
- Teachers know the subjects they teach and how to teach those subjects to students.
- Teachers are responsible for managing and monitoring student learning.
- Teachers think systematically about their practice and learn from experience.
- Teachers are members of learning communities.

Each of the first five sections below begins with the NBPTS's definition for each proposition and is followed by an elaboration focused on elementary school science teaching.

We have added our own sixth proposition, which is discussed after those of the NBPTS:

- Teachers consider the social, ethical, and civic implications of their actions both inside and outside the classroom.

Teachers Are Committed to Students and Their Learning

National Board–certified teachers are dedicated to making knowledge accessible to all students. They act

on the belief that all students can learn. They treat
students equitably, recognizing the individual differences that distinguish their students one from the
other and taking account of these differences in their
practice. They adjust their practice, as appropriate,
based on observation and knowledge of their students'
interests, abilities, skills, knowledge, family circumstances and peer relationships.

Accomplished teachers understand how students develop and learn. They incorporate the prevailing theories of cognition and intelligence in their
practice. They are aware of the influence of context
and culture on behavior. They develop students' cognitive capacity and their respect for learning. Equally
important, they foster students' self-esteem, motivation, character, civic responsibility and their respect
for individual, cultural, religious and racial differences [National Board for Professional Teaching Standards, 1991, p. 13].

According to conventional wisdom, accepted by many teachers,
science is complex, difficult, and especially hard to learn. Professional elementary school teachers have a particular commitment to
dispel this myth, believing that all students can learn science if
given the appropriate opportunities. Acting on that belief, accomplished teachers are dedicated to and skilled at making science
knowledge and skills accessible to all students, while they acknowledge students' distinctive traits and talents.

Teachers recognize individual differences in their students
and adjust their practice accordingly. They know their students, their
likes and dislikes, and their learning style preferences. They recognize that students have different kinds of intelligence—linguistic,
musical, mathematical, spatial, kinesthetic, personal (Gardner,
1983)—and so their science learning will be developed and demonstrated in different ways.

Teachers use their specific understanding of students' interests, abilities, and prior knowledge constantly to decide how best to
tailor instruction. In their planning, they anticipate the concepts

and activities certain students may find problematic. Watching students engaged in scientific investigations, they look for signs of progress. Through careful monitoring and the use of a variety of indicators of student learning, they decide when to alter plans, work with individual students, or enrich instruction with additional examples, explanations, or activities.

Teachers understand how students develop and learn. They use their knowledge of individual and social learning theory and of child development theory to inform their decisions about how to teach. They know the concepts generated by social and cognitive scientists, such as the learner-centered psychological principles synthesized by the American Psychological Association (1991), and the implications for learning and instruction. Moreover, they integrate such knowledge with their personal theories of learning and development generated from their own practice. For instance, accomplished teachers know that old theories of learning based on the accumulation of factual information have given way to more complex theories of conceptual development. As Bruce Watson and Richard Konicek (1990, p. 682) point out: "Learners bring their idiosyncratic and personal experiences to most learning situations. These experiences have a profound effect on the learner's view of the world and a startling effect on their willingness and ability to accept other, more scientifically grounded explanations of how the world works." Effective teachers understand the concept of constructivism, which recognizes that learning is a process of constructing new understandings on the basis of prior knowledge and whatever new information can enhance or elaborate on that knowledge. Proficient teachers know that simply giving students new information will not cause them to learn it but that understanding students' current conceptions and building on or challenging those conceptions effectively promote learning (Driver, Guesne, and Tiberghien, 1985).

Furthermore, elementary school teachers know that their students need many concrete experiences before they can understand important scientific concepts. They need multiple ways of connecting their science learning to their real-life experiences. As Piaget suggested, concrete science experiences are particularly important at the K–6 level to provide the underpinnings for later more abstract learning expected at the high school and university levels.

In their understanding of the many dimensions of intelligence, teachers also recognize the ways in which intelligence is culturally defined. Accomplished teachers recognize that in a multicultural nation students bring to school a plethora of abilities and aptitudes that are valued differently by the community, the school, and the family. Because of this, some abilities relevant to science learning will be more or less developed and reinforced outside the classroom. For example, some cultures find disturbing the logical, linear unfolding of a scientific investigation, the distinction made by the dominant society between the natural and the supernatural world, and the use of natural substances for experimentation. Proficient teachers are tuned into the diversity among students and develop an array of strategies for working with it. This includes providing educational experiences that capitalize on and enlarge the repertoires of learning and thinking that students bring to school. For example, the life cycle of trees that grow next to city streets, sidewalks, and buildings is very different from the life cycle of trees in woods or forests, and students familiar with each environment can work from what they know best. At some later stage, they may want to exchange information with their peers living in a different environment. Or, as another example, students can learn about the pollutants most common in their environment, such as lead in paint or water for urban students and the residue from pesticides and fertilizers for students in rural areas. Again, they can learn from peers in other locations through electronic or written communication.

Effective teachers have been trained in multiculturalism. In addition to recognizing and building on the similarities and differences among their students based on their culture, class, and general social milieu, teachers are proficient in a number of other ways.

• *Ensuring fairness in student-teacher interactions.* Teachers are aware of the research that points out that teachers may have more interactions with male students and students who are white than they do with female students and students of color (American Association of University Women, 1992). They are proactive in their interactions with students rather than reactive. This is complicated because accomplished teachers do not treat all students alike. Instead, they respond to differences in students, carefully avoiding favoritism and countering potential inequalities. They use what little is known about effective practice with diverse groups of students while striving to learn about how best to accommodate differences.

- *Spotting bias and stereotyping in texts and instructional materials.* Once aware of the inaccuracy of bias and stereotyping in the materials, teachers can use the bias or stereotyping to increase student learning. Accomplished teachers supplement biased materials with those that more accurately portray the life situations, perspectives, and contributions of women and people of color.

- *Providing a wide range of role models to students.* Young people need to see others of their gender, race, or ethnic group positively portrayed. Effective teachers ensure such exposure through bulletin board displays, guest speakers, audiovisual materials, mentoring programs, and other instructional vehicles.

- *Identifying school policies or practices that negatively impact on students because of their gender, race, or ethnicity.* The deleterious effects of grouping, tracking, and retaining students have been well documented (Oakes, 1982). Effective teachers know the impact of a policy or practice on a student's academic performance as well as self-esteem and put forward strategies that support rather than thwart learning.

- *Establishing the kind of learning environment where* all *students learn science and understand its importance in their lives.* At every opportunity, effective teachers counter the myth that some students do not need or cannot learn science. They are advocates for their students and for science.

Teachers' missions extend beyond developing their students' cognitive abilities. Effective teachers are concerned with their students' self-esteem and motivation, the effects of learning on peer relationships, and the development of character, aspiration, and civic virtues. Elementary teachers convince students that they *can* do science, that scientific careers are worthy of consideration, and that the kinds of investigatory and decision-making skills and "habits of mind" (a particular manner of thinking that is further explained in

Chapter Five) developed in their science experiences have application in all aspects of their lives.

Teachers Know the Subjects They Teach and How to Teach Those Subjects to Students

> National Board–certified teachers have a rich understanding of the subject(s) they teach and appreciate how knowledge in their subject is created, organized, linked to other disciplines and applied to real-world settings. While faithfully representing the collective wisdom of our culture and upholding the value of disciplinary knowledge, they also develop the critical and analytical capacities of their students.
>
> Accomplished teachers command specialized knowledge of how to convey and reveal subject matter to students. They are aware of the preconceptions and background knowledge that students typically bring to each subject and of strategies and instructional materials that can be of assistance. They understand where difficulties are likely to arise and modify their practice accordingly. Their instructional repertoire allows them to create multiple paths to the subjects they teach, and they are adept at teaching students how to pose and solve their own problems [National Board for Professional Teaching Standards, 1991, p. 13–14].

Accomplished elementary teachers have a rich understanding of science and appreciate how scientific knowledge is created, organized, linked to other disciplines, and applied to real-world settings. Teachers in command of the subject of science understand its substance. They acknowledge that, while the factual information most people think of as science is subject to change or redefinition, there are a few powerful concepts that help explain the world and need to be developed by all students by the time they leave the elementary grades (Bybee and others, 1989). Teachers understand these concepts, which include cause and effect, systems, scale, and change, and they value them as outcomes for their students.

While there is growing consensus that the overarching concepts (or themes) of science should provide the framework for curriculum choices in elementary school, the concepts themselves are not the topic of study. Children should have opportunities to explore many different exemplifications of the themes. A child who has watched a mealworm change into a pupa and then a beetle, who has planted a seed and watched it grow into a mature fruit-bearing plant, who has observed the hatching of a chick, the appearance of a spider's egg sac, or the birth of a kitten will have a deepening understanding of the meaning of the term *cycle* in living things. Over time, if that same student comes to know that rocks erode into sand and sand may compress and heat to form rock and that in a closed terrarium water evaporates, condenses, and evaporates again, cycle will take on an additional meaning and dimension. Observing, reading, watching films, and doing activities in the science classroom may all contribute to a growing understanding of cycle. Accomplished teachers know that their students' past experiences and preferred modes of learning vary. They build on what each child already knows and design a science program that will contribute additional interesting and memorable examples; no matter what the examples might be, the children will end up with a reasonable notion of the concept of cycles.

Further, accomplished elementary teachers know and can use the skills of scientific reasoning that they are expected to foster in their students: posing questions, designing investigations, gathering and analyzing data, and drawing conclusions. They know, value, and demonstrate such scientific "habits of mind" as a desire for knowledge, skepticism, tolerance of ambiguity, and honesty (Bybee and others, 1989).

Teachers also command specialized knowledge of how to convey science to students. Knowledge of science is not synonymous with knowledge of the most appropriate ways to present science ideas to students through analogies, metaphors, experiments, demonstrations, and illustrations. Understanding how scientific concepts interplay with the minds of learners is at the heart of the knowledge and skill required to teach science. The list of skills required to teach responsively to children and responsibly to the content is vast. An elementary teacher might ask: Are there ways to engage first graders in meaningful study of astronomy, or is there something about space that is conceptually beyond very young children? What might fascinate third graders about machines, and what would be useful ways to have them investigate the concept of work? What are responsible ways to have upper-elementary students conduct investigations? What notions—some appropriate, some not—about evidence and knowing are fostered by different approaches to investigations?

Accomplished teachers of science are aware of the most common misconceptions held by students, the aspects that they will find most difficult, and the kinds of prior knowledge, experience, and skills that students of different ages typically bring to the learning of particular topics. For example, many children think that plant food (fertilizer) and water constitute a fern's daily diet. Conceptions such as this often interfere with the development of the concept of plants making their own food. Other common misconceptions relate to why the sun "goes down" at night, the concept of gravity, and how light relates to vision. There are many scientific topics for which little is known about children's ideas and ways of thinking. Accomplished teachers know how to discover their students' present understanding so that they can use it as a starting point for new learning experiences. They also know how to structure the new learning experiences so as to lead to actual change in the students' conceptions rather than just to the memorization of facts.

Common misconceptions very likely spring from children's everyday experiences. J. Preston Prather (1985), in his examination of how to overcome misconceptions about science, describes several studies that demonstrate the formation of sophisticated science misconceptions by young children based on observations of everyday experiences. The earth does not seem to move; it is the sun that appears to be moving across the sky. When second graders have their shadows traced on the playground blacktop at 11 A.M. and return two hours later to find that no matter how hard they try, they cannot "fit" into the eleven o'clock shadow, they are faced with an indisputable fact: something has changed. In seeking an explanation for the change, however, they are confronted with a dilemma: the sun seems to have moved, not the earth; yet they have been told that day and night and the shortening, lengthening, and direction changing of shadows are caused by the motion of the earth. Teachers need to be prepared to deal with this very predictable confrontation of "fact" and intuitive belief based on one's own experience. They need to know how to guide students in constructing more sophisticated concepts than their previous notions in order to help them understand the phenomenon they have observed and reconcile it to their everyday experience.

Prather's (1985) study of the literature suggests that traditional teaching techniques have little effect in overcoming students' misconceptions in science. Science activities require students to integrate aspects of knowledge into their habits of thinking. They help students think in a nonlinear way, approaching issues from different perspectives, weighing multiple criteria, and considering multiple solutions. In exemplary science classrooms, students have an opportunity to apply their understanding to problems never before encountered. Their science teachers appreciate the fact that such reasoning will develop through repeated, thematic, and conscious effort and that it takes time, perhaps an entire year.

To generate multiple paths to science knowledge and understanding, teachers know how to draw on a wide variety of instructional strategies and curricular resources, including primary sources, models, reproductions, textbooks, teacher's guides, videotapes, and computer software, to optimize their students' learning. They are committed to keeping abreast of the latest developments in curricular material, especially those made possible by new technologies.

Knowledge of science teaching embodies a way of reasoning through and solving the problems that arise in the daily work of teachers. In their approaches to these problems, teachers bring to bear their knowledge of students, *and* learning, *and* teaching, *and* science.

Teachers Are Responsible for Managing and Monitoring Student Learning

National Board–certified teachers create, enrich, maintain, and alter instructional settings to capture and sustain the interest of their students and to make the

most effective use of time. They are also adept at engaging students and adults to assist their teaching and
at enlisting their colleagues' knowledge and expertise
to complement their own.

Accomplished teachers command a range of generic instructional techniques, know when each is appropriate, and can implement them as needed. They
are as aware of ineffectual or damaging practice as
they are devoted to elegant practice.

They know how to engage groups of students
to ensure a disciplined learning environment, and
how to organize instruction to allow the schools' goals
for students to be met. They are adept at setting norms
for social interaction among students and between students and teachers. They understand how to motivate
students to learn and how to maintain their interest
even in the face of temporary failure.

Board-certified teachers can assess the progress
of individual students as well as that of the class as a
whole. They employ multiple methods for measuring
student growth and understanding and can clearly explain student performance to parents [National Board
for Professional Teaching Standards, 1991, p. 14].

In these days of the crowded elementary curriculum, where science
often is neglected, it is especially important for teachers to take
responsibility for managing and monitoring the learning of science.
To accomplish these tasks, teachers call on their pedagogical
knowledge related to the teaching and learning of science.

Teachers are mindful of their principal science objectives. In
planning for instruction, accomplished teachers clearly understand
what scientific concepts and principles can be developed through a
particular science unit. Activities are seen as a means to valued ends
that include not only content understanding but also the skills and
habits of mind to be developed by the activity. For example, fourth-
grade teachers whose science curriculum calls for the study of insect
life cycles have an understanding of science that allows them to
decide which organizing concepts or "big ideas" this topic illus-

trates. They decide which insects to use as examples on the basis of such criteria as insects common to the school location, insects that can be ordered and studied in the classroom, insects the students themselves choose to study, insects that exhibit different patterns of life cycles. In planning the study, the teachers look for opportunities for students to do as scientists do, that is, ask questions based on present knowledge, explore, discover and create, design experiments, and communicate the results of their investigations to their classmates or indeed the greater community. These teachers select activities that appeal to fourth graders, that call for active participation, and that are challenging while ensuring success. A luna moth breaking out of its chrysalis in the classroom after weeks of study and observation captures the fancy of students in a way no textbook description can match. Culturing a mealworm and raising it to the adult (beetle) stage, finding out what it prefers to eat, and discovering how it responds to touch or odors are experiences few fourth graders forget.

Teachers use multiple methods to meet their science goals. They pose questions, guide students' inquiry and explorations, demonstrate phenomena, and show the thematic and conceptual interconnections among and across topics. They lead discussions, probe students' thinking, and create authentic opportunities for inquiry and demonstration of learning.

In addition to these methods, teachers know other procedures for teaching science, such as outdoor experiences, simulations, conceptual mapping, and computer-aided learning. They know how to draw on a variety of resources for teaching science, including various media, older children, community sources, parents, and peers. Finally, accomplished teachers assess the strengths and weaknesses of the various methods in terms of students, groups, topics, and outcomes.

Teachers orchestrate science learning in group settings. They know how to manage groups by setting social guidelines for classroom interaction. Students are taught appropriate roles and responsibilities for their own learning in groups and independently. Discipline and management strategies reflect teachers' careful consideration of the goals, students, context, and their own values and experiences. Thus, teachers are able to select alternative organizational arrangements for the classroom, weighing the advantages and disadvantages of various classroom structures for teaching science. They continually pursue novel ways of organizing the classroom to reach the desired outcomes.

Teachers place a premium on student engagement in meaningful scientific activity. Science is an especially powerful subject for motivating student engagement by capturing students' minds and bodies. Proficient teachers build upon and stimulate student interest while also motivating students to engage in challenging work and to persist through temporary failure. The hands-on building of a bat house is more rewarding than merely reading about bats; but the project needs to be "minds-on," too, by including data collection on bat populations and the analysis of bats' relationships with the various insects (or plants) in their environment. Such authentic science projects engage students in activity similar to that of adult scientists.

Science learning takes practice. As articulated in *Science for All Americans* (American Association for the Advancement of Science, 1989, p.46): "Students cannot learn to think critically, analyze information, communicate scientific ideas, make logical arguments, work as part of a team, and acquire other desirable skills unless they are permitted and encouraged to do these things over and over in many contexts." Moreover, a desire to practice is usually motivated by a feeling of achievement or success. Skilled coaching is often necessary, however, for students to achieve success and move forward. Effective teachers help their students clarify and order what they already know and what they want to find out; they guide students' activities so that students can collect and analyze data relevant to their questions. Effective science teachers know how to design and adapt challenging activities and resources that provide ample occasion for their students to practice and succeed.

Ms. Popkin's fifth-grade class was studying forces and motion by using small cars and wooden boards for ramps. The students were quite sure the cars went faster and faster as they ran down the ramps; at least some children said they knew this, and sev-

eral groups agreed that it seemed like this was what happened. They wanted to prove it, however, and struggled to devise a convincing way to do so. One group put strips of cardboard at equal intervals along the ramp and listened for the "bump" sounds to find out whether the sounds came closer and closer together as the car went down the ramp. But the exercise wasn't really convincing.

Then Ms. Popkin talked to the district science coordinator, who suggested that she borrow from the local high school a computer and a device that measured the distance of an object to a sensor and recorded the distance on the computer screen. Ms. Popkin was concerned about her ability to use such a sophisticated device, but her high school colleague bolstered her confidence by demonstrating it to her one day after school.

Back in class, Ms. Popkin placed the sensor at the top of one of the ramps. When a car sat motionless right next to the sensor and time began running, a straight line appeared near the bottom of the computer screen. When the car was released, the line on the screen rose in a curve from lower left to upper right.

"If the car rolled down at the same speed, the line wouldn't curve," said one student. "I think the faster the car goes, the steeper the line will be. Let's use a string to lower the car down the ramp slowly and then a little faster to see if this is true."

Sure enough, the slower the car, the flatter the line.

"Now, if we look at the section of the line at the beginning and compare it with a section when the car is almost at the bottom, if it's steeper at the

*end, it means the car really did go faster and
faster," exclaimed another student.*

*Ms. Popkin had used technology as a tool
when her students needed it to answer a question
they could not answer using other means at their
disposal. Changes that occurred over very short
periods of time and were imperceptible to the un-
aided senses could be observed by means of a
"microbased laboratory," or computer and sensor.
Ms. Popkin's students had confronted a problem
that required them to call upon various skills and
ways of thinking. They were fortunate to have a
teacher who understood that there was no single
route to understanding and who embraced the
opportunity for students to solve a problem neither
they nor she had encountered before.*

Teachers regularly assess student progress in science. Proficient teachers can track what students are (and are not) learning
from the science activities they design. While teachers must assess
the entire group and make decisions accordingly, they find ways to
learn about each individual student's learning. They are careful
observers of children and use a variety of means (portfolios, videotapes, demonstrations, exhibitions, and so on) to measure student
progress in science. By continually assessing what students have
learned, teachers are able to provide feedback to students and their
parents. Perhaps even more important, they use assessment information to design appropriate learning experiences for their students
and help them toward success.

Teachers Think Systematically About Their
Practice and Learn From Experience

National Board–certified teachers are models of educated persons, exemplifying the virtues they seek to
inspire in students—curiosity, tolerance, honesty, fair-

ness, respect for diversity and appreciation of cultural differences—and the capacities that are prerequisites for intellectual growth: the ability to reason and take multiple perspectives, to be creative and take risks, and to adopt an experimental and problem-solving orientation.

Accomplished teachers draw on their knowledge of human development, subject matter and instruction, and their understanding of their students to make principled judgments about sound practice. Their decisions are not only grounded in the literature, but also in their experience. They engage in lifelong learning which they seek to encourage in their students.

Striving to strengthen their teaching, Board-certified teachers critically examine their practice, seek to expand their repertoire, deepen their knowledge, sharpen their judgment and adapt their teaching to new findings, ideas and theories [National Board for Professional Teaching Standards, 1991, p. 14].

Teachers not only assess their students' science learning but also engage in assessment of their own science teaching and its relationship to student learning. They pursue their own growth through workshops, professional reading, and discussions with colleagues, using these activities as springboards for professional inquiry. Simply put, teachers use research and outside experts as a source of tools and ideas for inquiry rather than as a source of rules for practice (Sparks and Simmons, 1988).

Teaching requires a commitment to and active pursuit of lifelong learning. As with many professions, the field of teaching is constantly expanding, adding new challenges while increasing the knowledge base of effective practice. Consequently, accomplished teachers continue to learn, experiment, and refine their abilities to make good judgments about the opportunities they provide for students.

This is particularly true in elementary school science, where new understandings of how children learn have influenced a wide array of new materials, programs, and approaches for teaching. The challenge for teachers is great: to grow constantly in their repertoire of strategies and materials while staying closely attuned to the needs of their students—and continually improving their abilities to make the most appropriate match. If this growth does not occur, the teachers may implement new materials but probably will not do so effectively (Cronin-Jones, 1991). To keep pace with changing science curricula, teachers' knowledge and repertoire must also be open to change.

Elementary teachers are continually making judgments that influence their students' science learning. They must often make compromises that balance competing demands. For example, a teacher may have to reconcile the district's demand that he or she cover a text or a series of science units with his or her commitment to an in-depth understanding of a few key science concepts. Like-wise, a teacher will have to balance attention to the learning of science process skills with important concepts and principles neces-sary for developing scientific literacy. The commitment to teaching for deep understanding of a few scientific principles requires careful judgment on the part of teachers in their selection of the concepts and principles themselves, along with the topics and strategies through which these will be taught. Such situations require teachers to keep their commitment to their students' uppermost in mind when employing their professional knowledge of best prac-tice. While often more than one approach will work, a teacher's decision needs to be grounded in best practice and sound judgment.

Proficient teachers are aware that their experience is not al-ways the best teacher, so they search out opportunities to increase their knowledge. They solicit reactions to their teaching from stu-dents and parents. They invite colleagues to observe and discuss their teaching. They strive to make routine evaluations and super-visory conferences opportunities to reflect on their practice and learn about areas for improvement.

Accomplished elementary school teachers strive to stay cur-rent in their teaching fields. They seek out opportunities to enhance their knowledge of science content and teaching strategies not only through courses and institutes but also through less traditional sources, such as research laboratories, museums, and other science facilities. They might participate in research themselves, both scientific and classroom oriented, and find avenues to share the results. They conduct both formal and informal investigations to better understand their students' learning, while at the same time modeling the strategies and attitudes of inquiry for their students.

Elementary teachers, then, exhibit the same habits of mind about their own work that they hope to instill in their students in the pursuit of science, including curiosity, skepticism, honesty, respect for others' opinions, patience, respect for evidence—and a touch of humor.

Teachers Are Members of Learning Communities

National Board–certified teachers contribute to the effectiveness of the school by working collaboratively with other professionals on instructional policy, curriculum development and staff development. They can evaluate school progress and the allocation of school resources in light of their understanding of state and local educational objectives. They are knowledgeable about specialized school and community resources that can be engaged for their students' benefit, and are skilled at employing such resources as needed.

Accomplished teachers find ways to work collaboratively and creatively with parents, engaging them productively in the work of the school [National Board for Professional Teaching Standards, 1991, pp. 14-15].

Although teaching is commonly viewed as providing learning experiences for students, the work of teachers often does, and definitely should, reach beyond the classroom to wider communities of learning. The knowledge and skills of good teachers are most fully utilized when they (1) collaborate among themselves to improve the effectiveness of the school beyond their individual classrooms and (2) engage parents and others in the community in the education of young people.

Collaboration among elementary teachers is especially important for science teaching and learning. Teachers bring their individual strengths and preferences to teaching, and they work in such a way that each child benefits from a combination of their talents. Teachers who love science can profitably work with those who love language, or those who love mathematics or social studies, to bring their students a curriculum rich in meaning for their everyday lives, unplagued by artificial half-hour segments that separate the study of different content.

By being "closest to the customer," professional teachers play a proactive and creative role as they analyze and construct curriculum, coordinate instruction, contribute to the professional development of their peers and novice teachers, and participate in policy decisions that support the strongest possible learning community. Working on science curriculum teams, coordinating theme- or problem-focused instructional units, helping design science material support systems, and becoming "on-site" experts for particular science programs or approaches are all ways in which elementary teachers create their own learning communities. They provide continuity and equity for their students from class to class and grade to grade. Such activities require teachers to have a broad understanding of learning and optimal learning experiences, as well as collaborative and interpersonal skills.

Viewing the world beyond the school as part of students' learning community is critical for effective science teaching. Teachers share with parents the education of their students. As partners, they help parents support their children's learning through the development of curiosity, questioning, and wonder at the workings of the natural world. Teachers seek to understand from parents their students' individual experiences, are sensitive to differences in the cultures and family life of their students, and base learning experiences on these backgrounds.

Teachers also draw heavily on community resources in the teaching of science. Zoos, museums, parks, and botanical gardens enrich children's experiences with the natural world. Science labs, businesses, and industries demonstrate how science knowledge is developed and used and exemplify the variety of careers available to students. Environmental and health-related agencies further impress upon young people how science affects their lives. Teachers make creative use of community resources to enrich students' science learning.

Teachers Consider the Implications of Their Actions

In addition to thinking about the immediate sense students are making out of the content being taught, accomplished teachers ask themselves what social lesson is being taught that might eventually shape the way that students participate in a democratic society. They use the scientific habits of mind that are part of their science objectives to teach important social values.

Teachers know that the science learning experiences they develop for their students teach more than the scientific principles involved. In a lesson on condensation, for example, students learn not only how the phenomenon works but also how to think critically about the evidence, sift through it, draw conclusions, and test or question their conclusions. In this process, the teacher has the opportunity to help students see how they can take various versions of physical events and begin to build an understanding of apparently disparate observations. As they sift this "evidence," students can begin to draw conclusions about the events and those who are reporting them.

Experiencing situations that typically arise in science can contribute to students' critical thinking. Students can role-play scientists who conduct the same experiment and report conflicting results. As they consider each set of evidence, they begin to see that their own understanding is enhanced and expanded through the interaction. By sharing evidence and discussing it, students learn that accepting only one point of view without considering others is limiting and narrow. In this way, science becomes a powerful vehicle for encouraging students to question prevailing assumptions and to help them think for themselves.

A key to developing civic responsibility and ethical-social action relates to students' acceptance and understanding of cultures different from their own. Such differences may involve gender, race, class, religion, exceptionality, ability, or ethnicity. As already noted, science teachers make a point of honoring the contributions of diverse groups and work to free curriculum content of biases and stereotypes. Science teachers must be vigilant about students' beliefs that some social groups are less worthy than others. When such beliefs are expressed, effective teachers ask students to use scientific reasoning to support their hypotheses about why certain groups are not thriving in this society. The expression of mere opinion without analysis and investigation is challenged by professional teachers, whether or not the incident occurs during science instruction.

Elementary teachers recognize that science teaches habits of mind that are useful for those who function within a country whose system relies on citizens making informed choices and interacting in respectful ways with those who appear to have views different from their own. True knowledge of science implies an evaluation of activities carried out in the name of science and a pattern of questioning to understand the ramifications of such activities (Kyle, 1991).

The Compleat Teacher

Teachers who know, value, and use their understanding of science, student learning, and exemplary science teaching are invaluable to the elementary school classroom. The profound contribution of these teachers can be appreciated in the development of young people who have a budding understanding of how the natural world works and, perhaps more important, have a love and appreciation for future science learning.

The characteristics of effective science teaching discussed in this chapter clearly suggest that skilled teachers of science possess a rich, complex, and dynamic set of knowledge and skills. These include not only subject matter knowledge and knowledge about learners, curriculum, and assessment but an understanding of how content, psychology, and curriculum are transformed into teachable lessons. Lee S. Shulman (1987, p. 320), who has been immersed in the study and improvement of teacher education, has called the ability to make these transformations *pedagogical content knowledge*, "that special amalgam of content and pedagogy that is uniquely the province of teachers, their own special form of professional understanding."

Yet these aspects of teaching tell only part of the story, because a teacher's responsibilities, while directed toward the classroom, extend well beyond it. Teachers communicate with each other and with other professionals to share ideas, insights, and experiences; they regularly help mentor and induct new teachers into the profession; they participate in the design of instructional materials. Considering the broad range of a teacher's responsibilities, Shulman (1987, p. 319) has written: "our question should not be, Is there really much one needs to know in order to teach? Rather, it should express our wonder at how the extensive knowledge of teaching can be learned at all during the brief period allotted to teacher preparation." The poor preparation that most practicing and prospective elementary school teachers have been given in science compounds the problems that new teachers face in teaching science.

The idealized portrait of the exemplary teacher of science in the elementary grades painted in this chapter poses major challenges to preservice programs. What science experiences provide a sound foundation for the beginning teacher? How much time is needed for developing all the teaching skills expected of the elementary school teacher, even when new to teaching? And what should be the content and the organization of preservice courses? What elementary classroom experiences need to be built into methods courses? How should science and science methods courses be linked to create a successful program? If current teacher education practices in these areas are ineffective, how must they be changed? The next four chapters begin to address these questions.

4

Educating Prospective Teachers in Science: A New Vision

Once there is clarity about what elementary school teachers need to know and be able to do to teach science effectively, the next step is to design preservice programs that will provide the foundation for that knowledge and those abilities and help teachers develop them further throughout their career. We have chosen to describe a vision for such programs in three separate chapters. Chapter Four develops a vision of how elementary school teachers should be prepared in science. Chapter Five deals with the development of science content knowledge. Chapter Six discusses the development of pedagogical knowledge and skills. (Although we treat content knowledge and pedagogical knowledge in separate chapters, we are not suggesting that they ought to be separated in the preservice program itself; neither are we arguing that they should necessarily be combined.) Chapter 7 discusses the issue of program design. In it, we argue that an effective preservice program is not merely a collection of courses, even good ones; a preservice program must be more than the sum of its parts.

Before turning to the development of science content knowledge, we want to reemphasize the idea that runs throughout this book: learning happens when an involved learner confronts his or her current understanding of a concept and actively works to construct a new or better understanding. The notion that learning is active construction of knowledge rather than simple absorption of information is an essential concept for new teachers and is linked to a set of skills and strategies that they must acquire in order to help their students learn. However, the notion is also relevant to the design of teacher education programs in that it requires science and teacher education faculty to develop learning experiences for pre-service teachers that are quite different from traditional campus courses. Prospective teachers have just as much need for such con-structivist approaches as do their future students. The idea that learners are actively engaged in constructing their own knowledge also influences how learning experiences are combined to form a "program."

The issue of prior conceptions, for example, can illustrate one part of this idea. The research literature in science education in the last decade demonstrates a growing understanding of the effect of children's prior conceptions on their learning of science (Driver, Guesne, and Tiberghien, 1985). Young children appear to create their own theories and explanations about natural phenomena and how the world works. The reason why it is hotter in summer than winter is simple, they think. The earth must be closer to the sun in summer. After all, what child has not experienced the heat of a campfire or a stovetop burner and the result of coming too close? Even when confronted with data and a theory that offer an alterna-tive and more precise explanation, many cling to old notions.

What is now dawning is an understanding that, in a quite analogous way, the prior experiences of preservice teachers can dras-tically affect their notions of what ought to be taught and how it ought to be taught (Brousseau and Freeman, 1984; Feiman-Nemser, McDiarmid, Melnick, and Parker, 1988; Weinstein, 1989, 1990). Teachers construct knowledge about teaching in the same way that children make sense of their surroundings. As early as 1977, David R. Olsen found that preservice teachers often hold beliefs about teaching and learning that arise from commonsense knowl-edge, not from what they learn in science methods courses. These beliefs appear to be based on well-established, idiosyncratic memo-ries of previous teachers, former teaching and learning experiences, and childhood events. Taken together, these experiences and memo-ries have been labeled "teacher role identity" (Crow, 1087; Jasala-vich, 1992) and serve as a filter through which preservice teachers view the act of teaching.

Moreover, many preservice teachers fail to change their teacher role identity to incorporate the new ideas and methods acquired through pedagogy courses. One possible reason is that most preservice teachers have been successful in a system that values memorization and reproduction of ideas, not critical thinking and problem solving. Fourteen or more years of reinforcement of these ideas are difficult to overcome. Thus it is not surprising that many believe that teaching science is telling students what they need to know and view hands-on, reflective science as but one optional method they can use (Dana and Parsons, 1991). The end result has been science taught as it was learned—as lecture, reading, and only occasional laboratory experience or thoughtful discourse.

If teacher education is to change preservice teachers' conceptions of good science teaching, it must begin with what these individuals know and believe. Recognition of this fact requires that teacher education experiences be viewed as an opportunity to change preservice teachers' conceptions of teaching. This means that program experiences must identify and challenge college students' previously held, commonsense understandings about what teaching in an elementary classroom should be (Loucks-Horsley and others, 1989). To ensure this, programs must be designed as a whole, with overarching principles, such as teachers making sense of learning and teaching through guided experiences. Moreover, programs must challenge prospective teachers' beliefs that good teaching involves mesmerizing students with interesting lectures or keeping students busy quietly filling in worksheets. It also means that an instructor's notion of what constitutes good practice will probably not be shared by all students. As Sheila M. Jasalavich (1992, p. 31) states, "science educators should not assume their (own) understandings of statements such as 'hands-on science' and 'teacher as facilitator' are shared by their students."

The need for understanding preservice teachers' prior conceptions is just one implication of the idea of learning as the active construction of knowledge. There are implications as well for the way learning experiences are structured. The following vignette (stimulated by Shymansky, 1992) illustrates how a preservice teacher might learn to teach a science unit using a "constructivist" view of learning. Note that the actual course used to illustrate this idea combines science content and science pedagogy—one possible structural configuration for preservice programs.

Rick's science methods course was part of his preparation to teach elementary school. He was skeptical about this course at first because he'd heard it was being taught in a whole new way by a team of professors from the education and science departments. The syllabus showed no familiar list of lectures and labs covering various content topics. Instead, the class was divided into research teams, and the semester began with a meeting of Rick's team with a research biologist and an education professor.

At their first meeting, Rick learned that he was going to be a researcher. Expecting to be asked to choose a topic in biology, he was surprised to learn that the focus of the research was to be elementary students and that the research question was, What do elementary students think or know about how plants make food? Rick spent a week in a fifth-grade classroom interviewing students, asking them to describe how they thought plants make food, and getting them to draw their ideas. As they drew pictures and diagrams about relationships between plants and the sun and the rain and the soil, they explained their drawings and Rick took notes.

Rick carefully recorded his data. He also kept a journal in which he noted his reactions and feelings about the information-gathering process. At the end of a week, he and the three other students on his team met with the scientist and the education professor to share and make sense of their data. Rick expressed his astonishment at the range of ideas expressed by the fifth graders he had inter-

viewed. He learned that to one child plant food
meant the green stuff his father mixes in water and
pours on the plants in the house and garden once
every two weeks. This child "knew" that plants need
to be fed just like people do. Another child "knew"
that the sun makes food for plants, which the plants
can then give to animals. On probing, this child ad-
mitted that he wasn't quite sure how this works.
One girl said she knew how plants make food because she planted carrots and beans in a little
garden beside her house last year and then she ate
the carrots and the beans. But she wasn't sure how
the seeds turned into the vegetables. She guessed it
has something to do with the dirt.

　　　Rick was fascinated by what he learned from
these children. And it forced him to examine his
own understanding of how plants make food. What
did he really know? How and where did he get this
knowledge? He was sure photosynthesis was a key
process. But what could he remember about photosynthesis from his high school biology course? He
remembered some cycle, the Krebs cycle, and that it
was a nightmare memorizing it for the big test.
What were all those arrows exiting a circular path,
like roads branching from a rotary? What was the
point of it all anyway?

　　　At that point, his science professor took over
and Rick began a study of plant physiology with
laboratory investigations, readings, lectures, and
discussions designed for adult learning. As Rick
learned about photosynthesis, he was not only
thinking about his own learning but keeping in mind
what fifth graders think about plants making food.
He sought to understand the principles and details
of plant physiology well enough to choose a small

number of big ideas that could anchor the study of plants he knew he would work on with fifth graders in a month. He kept in mind that he would have to select activities that would be engaging and convincing to fifth graders. While he realized that the laboratory investigations in his college science course were inappropriate for elementary students, he reflected on what elements of hands-on investigations seemed likely to result in lasting learning, whether one was an adult learner or a child.

As he learned what the scientific community knows about plants and carbohydrate synthesis, Rick thought about the concepts fifth graders hold that contradict scientific explanations. He began to plan a strategy for presenting strong evidence on a fifth-grade level that would deepen his students' understanding of the process and its place in their own daily lives.

At the end of the third week, Rick was deeply engaged in his study of photosynthesis, his study of how children learn, and the process of learning about learning. His journal entries reflected his growing understanding that, if his students were to carry away a thorough understanding of science, he must be the kind of teacher his professor had been for him in this course. He must structure his programs so that students become investigators, asking their own questions, seeking answers for themselves, but with their classmates and teacher as co-searchers, active listeners, and helpers. He hoped he could help students learn science content that seemed meaningful and useful, just as learning about photosynthesis was meaningful and useful to him in the context of his science methods course.

In one journal entry, Rick noted: "I can't tell

whether I'm learning science or how to teach
science, or about my own learning or kids' science
learning, or what. It's all intertwined and packed to-
gether. And it's beginning to make sense. I think I'll
be ready to plan and teach that fifth-grade plant
study next month."

Figure 4.1 graphically illustrates the preceding vignette, summarizing the various steps Rick went through in his science methods course. It divides the process into three sections, each of which begins with a question, uses inquiry to develop answers, and ends with a demonstration of understanding before proceeding to the next step. In this instance, the process begins with the question of what children think about how plants make food and ends with lesson plans for a unit entitled "Plants and Food." Although the content in each step is specific to the vignette, the model can accommodate a wide range of subject matter. Furthermore, the sequence of the sections can change, depending on the nature of the individual program. For instance, instead of starting with the question of what children think about a topic, the process could begin with students investigating the content in its own right in a science content course, and then in a subsequent science methods course inquiring into how children view the topic. Alternatively, students taking the content and the methods courses during the same semester could pursue both questions simultaneously. The common denominator in all the permutations of this model is that students complete the process by developing methods of teaching the topic and that science content and pedagogy are coordinated enough for connections to be drawn between the two courses (if they are separate). A further element, as we discuss in Chapters Six and Seven, is the opportunity for preservice teachers to try out the methods they have developed on students of the age they expect to teach, reflect on the results they obtain, and—just as scientists do—revise and refine their approaches.

Figure 4.1. Program Elements for Elementary Teacher Preparation in Science.

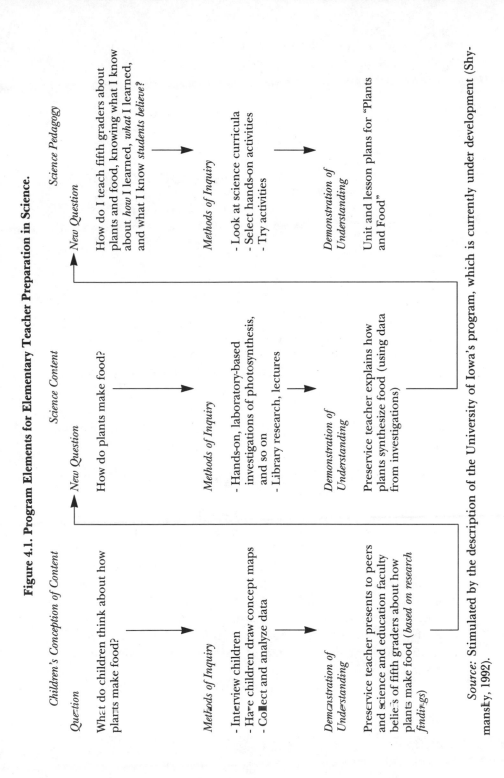

Children's Conception of Content

Question

What do children think about how plants make food?

Methods of Inquiry

- Interview children
- Have children draw concept maps
- Collect and analyze data

Demonstration of Understanding

Preservice teacher presents to peers and science and education faculty beliefs of fifth graders about how plants make food (*based on research findings*)

Science Content

New Question

How do plants make food?

Methods of Inquiry

- Hands-on, laboratory-based investigations of photosynthesis, and so on
- Library research, lectures

Demonstration of Understanding

Preservice teacher explains how plants synthesize food (using data from investigations)

Science Pedagogy

New Question

How do I teach fifth graders about plants and food, knowing what I know about *how* I learned, *what* I learned, and what I know *students believe?*

Methods of Inquiry

- Look at science curricula
- Select hands-on activities
- Try activities

Demonstration of Understanding

Unit and lesson plans for "Plants and Food"

Source: Stimulated by the description of the University of Iowa's program, which is currently under development (Shymansky, 1992).

5

Developing Science
Content Knowledge

Chapter Three argues that the elementary school teacher needs to have a good foundation of science knowledge, skills, and habits of mind to create appropriate science learning environments for children. This chapter elaborates on the argument, suggesting characteristics of science course work, science research experiences, and other learning opportunities that prepare teachers with respect to their content knowledge.

What Is Science?

Most prospective elementary school teachers, as noted, have an incomplete view of science, seeing it as a body of information (facts, concepts, laws, theories) that the scientific community has developed and students need to learn. Teachers (preservice and often those already practicing) ignore the view of science as a way of understanding the world that uses certain modes of inquiry, rules of evidence, and ways of formulating research questions. Unfortunately, the view of science as a body of information is pervasive. The preservice curriculum, instead of reenforcing this view, needs to remedy it.

On occasion—in college science courses, in high school, and even in elementary school—prospective teachers are ostensibly taught how science is done by scientists, that is, how scientific knowledge is created. This, they are told, is the "scientific method," which they religiously follow in their laboratory experiments and pass on to their elementary school students. In beginning science courses, this method is often described as a series of steps consisting of observation, hypothesis formation, prediction, and testing—the inductive method as devised by Sir Francis Bacon in the seventeenth century.

Since then, it has become clear that scientists think and know in a variety of ways, and their methods seldom fall into a neat set of steps that begin with observation and end with hypothesis confirmation. Science tends to act like a feedback loop in which new information and current ideas are tested against old ideas. If the new ideas work, the old ideas are modified. Furthermore, scientists employ several different strategies, or ways of knowing, to understand nature. Prospective teachers need to be aware of these as they grapple with the nature of the science they want their students to learn.

One strategy is to carry out experiments to confirm or disprove a hypothesis. A famous early experiment, by Judge Dudley in 1724, concerned the belief that genetic characteristics of plants are passed on through their roots (Visser, 1986). Two different species of corn were planted in two situations: separated by a stream, preventing interaction between the roots, and separated by a tall solid fence, preventing interaction above ground. It turned out that the offspring of the corn separated by the stream had characteristics of both parent types, whereas the offspring of the corn separated by the fence did not, thus disproving the root theory.

Another strategy is to carry out an analysis relative to some standard, for example, to determine what an unknown substance is, one can observe how it reacts with known substances and compare the pattern of reactions to known patterns, thus identifying the substance.

Sometimes indirect measures must be used. Thomson was able to prove the existence of the electron, even though he could not directly observe a single electron and measure its properties. He deflected the rays in a cathode-ray tube in magnetic and electric fields, measured the bending of the path of the cathode rays, and then calculated the charge to mass ratio of the particles making up the rays—the hypothesized electrons.

Stephen J. Gould (1986) explains that Charles Darwin's major writings may be thought of as explications of ways of thinking and knowing that are quite different from carrying out experiments. Darwin (1881) wrote a treatise on worms that demonstrates belief in a homogeneous nature and the power of extrapolating as a mode of scientific inquiry. After observing the worms in his garden and how they mixed the soil as they burrowed through it, Darwin extended that observation to theorize about how many worms there might be in the world and how much they may have affected the development of soils.

Darwin's (1842) treatise on coral reefs shows how one can take data spread over space, order it, and reconsider it as representing data spread over time. After visiting many islands in the Pacific Ocean, with their various reefs and atolls, Darwin became convinced that he was seeing the different stages of the development of atolls. He explained that reefs first grow along the shores of small volcanoes, and as the volcanoes subside and disappear, a circular reef (atoll) is left behind. No scientist has ever seen the actual creation of an atoll, but each of the stages can be found independently on various islands. Putting them into a sequence was Darwin's brilliant idea.

Astronomers regularly use this type of thinking to create sequences of stars that are thought to show the stages in the evolution of a single star. Much of current knowledge about planetary evolution comes from thinking about solar system planets as a sequential array illustrating the stages of development over time. Classification of objects into arrays is another way of developing scientific knowledge.

If elementary school teachers are to introduce their students to science, they themselves need to experience the variety of methods that science uses to make sense of the world. Different science disciplines use different methods. One way to expose prospective teachers to several methods is to require them to take courses in several different sciences, for example, three. If science courses are developed to be interdisciplinary, however, the emphasis should not be on how many courses are taken; instead, the courses should include several ways of knowing in science. Indeed, there is little evidence that simply the number of science credits taken has much effect on teacher performance (Yager and Penick, 1990).

Although many different scientific methods exist, they all share these features: asking questions of nature, creating protocols (experiments, observations) to answer those questions, carrying out the protocols, evaluating the data and looking for patterns, formulating conclusions, and reporting results. Furthermore, scientists almost always skip around when addressing these things. Reporting may suggest new experiments. Experiments may force new questions of nature. Science is not a straightforward, linear process. Effective science education for prospective teachers gives them experiences in using these six features and learning to make predictions based on science knowledge and evidence.

What Science Should
Prospective Elementary Teachers Learn?

University professors responsible for designing science course work must think about the science that prospective elementary school teachers will study as being an introduction to lifelong science learning, not to being a science major. Whatever course work these students take as undergraduates may well be their last formal science education. This means that one goal of science education for prospective elementary school teachers, and indeed for all students, must be to equip them to be self-educating in science. Robert E. Yager and John E. Penick's (1990) study of least and most effective science teachers showed that the most effective teachers constantly sought out new information, materials, and strategies.

Observing classroom teachers in elementary schools makes one thing very clear: they are engaged in much decision making while being immersed in an ever-changing world. Some of the "facts" of science will be modified or of lesser importance in the future. Teachers need to learn science in such a way that they can fit new knowledge and new ideas into their understanding of the world. Prospective teachers need to be taught how to update what they know and how to keep current.

Science helps build understandings of the world of nature and the human world. Major concepts that undergird science, such as cause and effect, continuous and discontinuous properties, systems analysis, and extrapolation, might at first appear to lie only in the domain of science; yet they also are powerful tools for analyzing the world outside science. What are the causes of change in human history? Can one consider one thing at a time, or are there many interdependencies that one must take into account? How far can one dare extrapolate from anecdotal evidence? These are all important ways of thinking about life in general, not just natural phenomena.

A few major concepts can form the foundation of science education for prospective elementary school teachers. In *The Liberal Art of Science,* the American Association for the Advancement of Science (1990, p. 21) notes that "certain ideas transcend disciplinary boundaries and are essential to understanding intellectual relationships among all the disciplines of science." The California Science Framework adopted a similar approach, developing six concepts that overlap the AAAS concepts. The major AAAS integrative concepts are as follows (adapted from the American Association for the Advancement of Science, 1990, pp. 22–24):

1. *Causality and consequence.* Cause and effect are absolutely fundamental ideas of science, and much of the activity of science is discriminating among causality, contingency, correlation, and coincidence.
2. *Scale and proportion.* Understanding scale and proportion requires mathematical competence. An appreciation of scale and proportion is needed to deal with cosmic and atomic dimensions, geological and cosmological time, and other large and small phenomena.
3. *Dynamic equilibrium.* Systems of dynamic equilibrium are very common in nature. Related concepts are synergism, feedback loops, steady state, and nonequilibrium.
4. *Change and evolution.* The world is in constant change. Most natural systems evolve over time, and it is important to understand the nature of change and evolution.

We do not mean to imply that science instruction, either for prospective teachers or for elementary school students, should start with these or similar themes. Rather, it must move from discussion and in-depth investigation of relatively simple-seeming topics to an eventual development of some of the key concepts and how they illuminate and connect major fields of science. Hence, not every college science course will pay equal attention to each of the integrative concepts, but the curriculum as a whole should address all of them as capstones to students' science learning. Even then, it would probably not be wise to use the concepts as the principal headings of a curriculum (for example, a course or unit on dynamic equilibrium). It would be better to use them as explicit explanatory mechanisms within and across disciplines. Thus, when a student studies chemistry, the emphasis should be on understanding the role of causality and consequence, scale and proportion, dynamic equilibrium, and change and evolution when dealing with chemical explanations of the world. So, too, should the biological, physical, and earth sciences emphasize these integrative concepts.

The specific content and strategy of science programs for preservice teachers should be dictated by local needs and resources. The test of whether there is proper breadth and depth of science content is in the understanding of integrative concepts on the part of students. Good programs will produce prospective teachers who can view their own world in scientific ways, most especially including these ideas. Equipped in this way, they will be able to help their elementary school students develop scientific ways of thinking and knowing.

Understanding science concepts and developing scientific ways of thinking are two outcomes for science experiences. In addition, teachers need to develop the scientific habits of mind that ought to form part of their goals for the science learning of their students (Bybee and others, 1989). Although these habits of mind should pervade all phases of scholarship, science illustrates them particularly well (adapted from Bybee and others, 1989, p. 51):

1. *Desiring to know*. Recognizing that science is a way of knowing and having a disposition toward knowing and understanding the world are important for elementary science education.
2. *Being skeptical*. A part of this attitude is recognizing the appropriate time and place to be scientifically skeptical and to hold a disposition that authoritarian statements and self-evident truths can be questioned.

3. *Relying on data.* Obtaining and ordering data are the basis for explanations of natural phenomena. Relying on data also means rigorously testing ideas and respecting the facts as they are accrued.

4. *Accepting ambiguity.* Data are seldom clear and compelling; and scientific information seldom, if ever, proves something. New questions and problems arise out of ambiguity.

5. *Being willing to modify explanations.* As data suggest different explanations of objects or events, one must be willing to change one's original explanations.

6. *Cooperating in answering questions and solving problems.* Cooperation is important to the scientific enterprise. An individual can seldom know enough on his or her own.

7. *Respecting reason.* Scientists value patterns of reasoning that lead from data to conclusions and eventually to construction of testable hypotheses.

8. *Being honest.* Data should be presented as they are observed, not as the investigator thinks they ought to be. Sooner or later dishonesty will be exposed.

How Should Preservice Teachers Learn Science?

Much of what happens in science programs for prospective elementary school teachers can mimic good science itself. University students should be doing things in their programs that parallel the activities of scientists: they should *do* science, not learn about science. Too often, science courses are taught like history lessons, recapitulating for students in lecture form or through the repetition of key experiments the development of scientific knowledge about a topic, say, the structure of an atom. Doing science does not mean learning about past scientific achievements (although this has a legitimate place in the curriculum); it means that preservice teachers must be given opportunities to behave like scientists. Further, behaving like real scientists at work is a convincing way to show that science is not always linear. The best research plans must be modified as the work goes forward; often there are iterations that lead to new questions different from the ones originally asked. Final reports almost never reveal the deadends, wrong turns, and stop-and-go progress. Preservice teachers need to learn the realities of day-to-day science.

Often, the topic chosen for investigation will relate to subject matter germane to the elementary school science curriculum, but it must be treated at a level appropriate to adult learners. Our study of preservice programs indicates that, of those programs in which science courses were specially designed for prospective elementary school teachers (about a third of all programs surveyed), the great majority adopted this approach (see the Appendix). At times, however, the topic may be chosen because it appeals to adult students' interests, lends itself readily to investigation, and provides an excellent opportunity for students to experience both the hard work and joy of doing science. Prospective teachers should be taught adult content and then taught how to use it to design content appropriate to the grade level they plan to teach.

As shown in the vignette that follows, a science professor might modify a traditional science course to make it appropriate for prospective teachers but keep the content and work at a high level of intellectual rigor. The changes described alter the way the content is taught, not the actual content presented. Prospective teachers need not necessarily have a course that is developed for them. They need science courses that present science as a dynamic and inquiry-based field.

John had spent a good chunk of the summer preparing his syllabus for his general biology course. This year, in addition to pre-med and science majors, some of his students would be preparing to teach elementary school science. A research group at his university had just released the results of a study of undergraduate teaching. He was intrigued to read that students seemed both satisfied and successful when they were in small interactive classes, such as foreign language classes, or when study groups were part of the structure of the course. This in no way described his series of lectures on the latest findings in biological sciences and his laborato-

ries that challenged students to duplicate some classic experiments in biology.

While his course had seemed to prepare those already disposed to study science for what was to come, John knew he was also losing students who could not keep pace with the work. He wondered if the pace and content of his course would be appropriate to prospective elementary school teachers. Maybe a simplified course or one that emphasized activities for elementary students would serve them better.

Troubled by the need to make one course meet the needs of several groups of students, John asked a member of the education department to have lunch with him at the faculty club. "Shouldn't these students be learning science activities for first, or third, or fifth grade?" he asked his colleague. "Why do they need to know the complexities of respiration or evolution? Their elementary students will never need to know all that detail."

His colleague replied: "When teachers have a firm grounding in scientific content, in biology, physical science, and earth science, they are more confident in their ability to make curricular choices for their students. I've observed that they also yearn for the security that flows from up-to-date, solid understanding of subject matter. They are adults. Teach them on the adult level, and let them make the decisions about what material is appropriate for a particular age child. They know how youngsters learn, and they know how to orchestrate a class."

Later, John recalled this conversation as he watched his students study their petri dishes of cultures of E.coli. He had challenged them to produce *a strain of the* E.coli *that would be resistant to the antibiotic erythromycin. They had learned how to cut DNA strands into sections by using enzymes and how to separate the samples by a technique called gel electrophoresis. Ethidium bromide had been added to the DNA, and his students now looked through their goggles at the gel illuminated by ultraviolet light. They seemed to be truly thrilled. It was always a beautiful sight to see those glowing fragments of DNA, some longer, some shorter. Now all those terms like* gene *and* DNA *and* base pairs *were real to his students, all of his students. And they themselves had done the manipulations. It had been as engaging for the ones planning a career in science as it had been for the others.*

However, making the DNA visible and differentiating one sample of DNA from another was not the end. Next, the students introduced the different fragments into cultures of E.coli *to see if they could produce strains that were resistant and nonresistant to various antibiotics. On this day, John listened to one pair of students exclaiming over the fact that they had managed to transform a strain of bacteria that was nonresistant to erythromycin into a resistant strain. And, what was more, they had been able to reproduce these bacteria once again.*

"So that's what cloning means!" exclaimed one of the pair of teachers-in-preparation. "And now I understand what they mean when they say your genes determine how you look and what you can become. If the DNA strand had been different, we probably wouldn't have gotten the bacteria to be resistant to the antibiotic."

"It's amazing and beautiful," replied the other member of the pair in a hushed tone.

When these adults who were preparing to be teachers begin their science lessons with their young students, they will not talk of DNA or gel electrophoresis or cloning or *E.coli*. But they will probably have a sparkle in their eyes when science time rolls around and enthusiastically invite their students to investigate the natural world. They will have a deeper understanding of why it is so important for youngsters to notice and appreciate the diversity of living things and the patterns to be found in nature. Like begets like, but not always exactly. Variation and change are also patterns in nature. Biotechnology, a currently lively area of research, no longer will be a mystery to these teachers. In fact, they know the basic techniques that are helping answer some of today's "hot" questions. They know that their students will undoubtedly be faced with questions scientists haven't even thought of yet but that their students can learn the techniques that can lead to answers. They can even be the ones who ask the important questions.

These adult students will have to grapple with the question of exactly what activities and specific topics will be developmentally appropriate for their elementary science classes. However, they will do so with the confidence that comes with a thorough understanding of some of the key topics in science and a knowledge of the processes and skills of scientific investigation rather than just a knowledge of either processes or content (Yager and Penick, 1990).

As the foregoing vignette indicates, doing science also means adopting a norm of teamwork. The image of the lone scientist at work in a remote laboratory is historically interesting, but more and more often in the modern world, teams of people do the science in a particular field. Scientists share their expertise and so, too, should preservice teachers in university science programs. They should do their learning in teams in which individual responsibilities change over time. One week Salim is the recorder and Mary is the leader, while Darla does the instrumental manipulations. For the next investigation, roles are exchanged. In this way, everyone practices and learns various skills.

Sheila Tobias has shown that successful programs in science education emphasize a sense of community. Faculty who design such programs pay attention to the culture of their institution, examining why science is difficult to learn in most universities. As

Tobias (1992, p. 19) notes: "What hinders students are the pace; the conflicting purposes of the courses (to, variously, provide an introduction, or lay a foundation for a research career, or weed out the 'unfit'); attitudes of their professors and fellow students; unexplained assumptions and conventions; exam design and grading practices; class size; the exclusive presentation of new material by means of lecture; and the absence of community—a host of variables that are not specifically addressed by most reforms."

Reform of the undergraduate science curriculum is only part of the equation. The other issues that Tobias raises must be addressed and solved as well. Some of the elements of successful programs identified by Tobias are open-ended, real laboratory problems, continuing projects, group work, peer counselors, student observers helping faculty, faculty as managers of change, peer mentoring, open access to laboratories and computers, and emphasis on the processes of learning and teaching. Her suggestions clearly intimate that it will not be sufficient to design new courses; success in preparing elementary science teachers will require new cultural values in the university.

Testing is another component of the undergraduate science course work that will need to change. It will do no good to adopt new programs if the final assessment of students does not reflect the wide variety of outcomes being emphasized. Examinations and other assessments that do not directly evaluate the knowledge, skills, and habits of mind emphasized in this book will be self-defeating. "Good" students know that the bottom line is determined by looking at how professors arrive at grades. This sort of student may remark: "Just *tell* me. Why should we do all these things in the laboratory without knowing whether we will get the right results? We had really good lectures in my high school courses, and I did really well on my achievement tests for college. If we spend as much time on every topic as we have on this DNA experiment, we won't have enough time left to learn all the other things I need to know to teach my students."

These remarks indicate that this student brings her successful high school experience to her college science course. The modes of assessment she has experienced have not prepared her for a real engagement with science or with the kind of learning that will enable her to teach science to young students. Testing and grading policies must reflect the comprehension of science as a way of knowing and understanding the major integrative concepts of science, and the acquisition of the important habits of mind. New ways of evaluating student accomplishments must be developed. These may include group grades, peer evaluations, portfolios, oral exams, presentations, short essays, and other innovative techniques that will capture the broadest range of science learning outcomes (Raizen and others, 1989).

Examples of Appropriate Science Learning Activities

This section presents examples of how three different topics might be taught in college science courses. No single example contains all of the integrative concepts, but each example is robust because it is real and promotes scientific inquiry. Although each example fits largely into one scientific discipline, it clearly overlaps with others, as it does with technological and societal issues.

Accelerated Erosion

Accelerated erosion often can be found locally; a rapidly growing gully is an excellent example, although landslides and slumps can also serve the purpose. When students are taken to such areas they can be asked (in teams) to gather observations about the anomaly. What is different in the landscape? Does it appear that some areas are undergoing more rapid erosion than others? Simple mapping techniques can show the extent of the erosion, and particular attention can be paid to what different types of phenomena can be observed: barren soil, exposed rocks, uprooted trees, piles of rock or sediment at the base of the slope, and so on.

Students can speculate about the "causes" of the erosion. Perhaps, for example, the slopes are in disequilibrium because of excessive runoff, oversteepening, or overloading. In any event, hypotheses can be created to explain the erosion and a scheme developed to ask nature about the causes. Has there been a change in runoff due to farming, or oversteepening of the slope due to construction? Are the materials present particularly susceptible to erosion? Additional observations can be made to test assumptions about the behavior of materials.

All of this leads to explanations that can be tested for their ability to predict the behavior of the slope or to explain the erosion that already has taken place. Reporting occurs as the work proceeds because people must communicate their ideas and observations to one another. At some point, closure must occur and a final report made of the newly acquired knowledge. The report could be presented in oral, written, poster, or some other form. Team presentations might make use of color slides, overhead transparencies, videotape, and other media.

This field investigation has value as an assignment because it includes several major integrative concepts, including equilibrium (static, dynamic, "thresholds"), properties of scale (cohesion, inertia), systems analysis (relationships of water, vegetation, soils, topography, humans), change (evolution of systems, reversibility), and cause and effect (necessary and sufficient causes). It is also valuable because it can be related to such other ideas in geology as entrainment of sediment, angle of repose, grain-size distribution, water-sediment interactions, and strength of materials. Moreover, the investigation may lead to questions that explore the interaction of science and society because the effects of human actions on natural systems and attendant consequences may be involved. Finally, the work being done by students relates to a real scientific problem.

The Physiology and Behavior of Dinosaurs

The physiology and behavior of dinosaurs are a fascinating subject to people of all ages. Making reasonable assumptions about what dinosaurs might have been like and testing those speculations are good illustrations of some of the ways that scientists think about the past. Here are just some of the questions that can be asked at the beginning of this learning activity: how can we know whether dinosaurs could run and jump? If they could run and jump, how fast and how far? The hypotheses that can be generated will result in a kind of reasoning by analogy. Is it sensible to think of dinosaurs as being similar (analogous) to modern-day animals and, if so, which modern animals? Are they similar to such large birds as emus and ostriches? Are they like elephants and giraffes? In what ways might they be similar, and in what ways might they be dissimilar? Can we think of dinosaurs (at the least, of their skeletons) as large machines that can be analyzed in engineering terms?

Given these types of questions and speculations, students can address assumptions about analogies and then go on to create possible explanations for dinosaur behavior. For example, some interesting relationships have been established between the size, shape, and cellular characteristics of dinosaur and mammal bones. These relationships have led some scientists to assert that some dinosaurs were warm-blooded (Thomas and Olson, 1980). Other interesting relationships have been established between the speed of dinosaurs and their leg length and stride length. For example, R. M. McNeill Alexander (1983, 1989) has been able to calculate the probable speed of some dinosaurs from Texas on the basis of a mechanical analysis of their stride length and size. Some of these ideas can be tested by looking at the students themselves. Who is fastest in the class? Can the fastest be predicted on the basis of leg and stride lengths? Given a set of data showing running speed and skeletal features, can one predict who is fastest? A visit to a local natural history museum might provide the opportunity to take skeletal measurements and predict relationships. All of this investigation can result in an evaluation of the best kind of modeling of how dinosaurs might have behaved. Students can work on this intriguing question by forming teams of researchers. Their work can be both library and laboratory based, just as it is for practicing scientists. Results can be reported by means of a variety of media.

This investigation is valuable because it includes such major integrative concepts as properties of scale (size, strength, inertia) and change (organic evolution). It can be directly related to such other concepts in biology as organic evolution, energy in organisms, and patterns of growth. It is a good example of how scientists deal with problems in which direct experimentation is impossible. There are no living dinosaurs that anyone can observe running. Reasoning by analogy is nevertheless a powerful way of thinking and knowing in science.

Water Pollution

Many areas of the country are experiencing pollution of groundwater and surface-water systems. The pollutants range from saltwater incursion due to the overpumping of coastal aquifers to highly localized toxic materials from badly engineered landfills to regional problems of agricultural chemicals to the deposition of air pollutants onto land surfaces. Part of a chemistry course can be organized in such a way that students create the protocol to find out what pollutants exist in their area. This involves choosing appropriate analytical techniques and determining how and where to sample. Students must also consider scale, precision and accuracy, and extrapolation. Once data are acquired, the problem becomes one of determining the importance of the pollutants and whether mitigation is warranted. This will further involve students not only in questions of human response to the pollutants but also in questions of how human life is valued in a democratic society. The technical feasibility and financial cost of mitigation, the ethics of more-than-zero tolerance for pollutants, and the politics of where money will come from for mitigation will all be important.

This type of activity can be used to help students understand that science alone seldom solves environmental problems. The class can role-play the problem of a local environmental protection agency that must decide on pollution limits, mitigation, and reclamation. Who will pay? And how much? Science and technology can contribute to the answers. A student panel acting as a government agency can address many of the critical links between science and public policy. Perhaps even more important, such discussions will make students examine carefully how scientists think about natural phenomena and information of import to the wider community. The students' science understanding will deepen as they struggle with questions about the use of scientific knowledge.

A Curriculum-Related Unit

Some undergraduate science instruction is likely to deal with content appropriate for the elementary school curriculum. Great care should be taken to ensure that such material is taught at an adult level, including an appropriate level of sophistication for any investigation. The following story illustrates how a common elementary school activity known as "batteries and bulbs" can be used to teach science at an adult level.

Maria walked into her physics lab with mixed feelings. She had avoided physics in high school because it seemed to be mostly math. Although she remembered about circuits and voltage and wattage from general science, she was still a little reluctant as she approached the first electricity lab. But when the lab instructor presented her with wire, battery, and bulb, she knew this was a different kind of course. The physics labs she had seen always had preset circuit boards and meters everywhere.

She and her partner, Brad, first tried connecting the tip of the bulb to the wire and connecting the wire to the battery. Brad, she noticed, handled the wire by the insulation because, as he said, he didn't want to get a shock. Try as they might, the light would not go on until they had put the metal tip of the bulb against the button on the battery and the wire from the back side of the battery to the metal screw portion of the light.

Maria and Brad might have stopped there, for they felt they now knew a lot more about electricity. But the next day in lecture, the professor asked a series of questions for which Maria and Brad had no answers; they had not tried various alternatives. Back to the lab they went. For the following day's class, they were armed with such observations as: "It doesn't seem to matter which end of the battery touches the metal tip of the bulb, but you must have a connection to both ends of the battery and both 'ends' of the bulb."

> *As Maria left class on Friday of the same week, she commented partly to herself and partly to Brad that this was the first time she felt she really understood what was meant by a circuit, let alone a complete circuit.*
>
> *A week later, Maria was even more surprised when she found out that she could take relatively few D cells in series and light a 40-watt household bulb. Her notion of the mathematics and the formula for voltage was that it would take about eighty D cells, yet there the bulb was lit, a little dimly perhaps, with about twenty cells. How was the professor going to explain that? she mused as she walked into class on Monday.*

This vignette is instructive for several reasons. First, it illustrates that students may remember concepts with a thin representation at a formal level. Such a representation often revolves around the familiar "plug and chug": put the numbers in the memorized formula and hope for the right answer; verify that answer in the lab by reading results off a meter in a circuit, with little relation to any real-world situation. In contrast, by starting the lab with familiar objects that students feel they should know about, the course develops an authentic reason for students' interest. Linking the lecture and recitation to the lab illustrates that the learning is integrated. Later work that includes relevant mathematics and the speculation that eighty cells would be needed to light the bulb indicates that learning should and can be at an adult level. While the future teachers may eventually teach "batteries and bulbs" to their own classes, the batteries-and-bulbs unit in their college course must go beyond material learned by elementary students and can utilize the abstract thinking skills college students possess if placed in a concrete context of real batteries and bulbs. College students can be stretched into the physics of abstractions and can learn in that context. Having strong real-world experiences will help them fit the abstractions into a conceptual web of solid understanding.

This example illustrates how a traditional topic can be

taught through lab experiences, lectures, and recitations that are interrelated and cause students to use the skills of science. Students can hypothesize in the lecture as well as in the lab; they can have concepts explained and put into context in the lab as well as the lecture. What matters is that the topics presented be intellectually stimulating for students at the college level and that they be chosen so as to allow students to perceive the connectedness of science.

Perhaps the most important lesson that prospective elementary school teachers can learn is that science can be exciting to do and valuable to their and their students' lives. If elementary school teachers are knowledgeable and enthusiastic about science, they can teach science well to their students. If they believe that science is dry, authoritarian, and irrelevant, however, they cannot possibly be good teachers of science. If they learn that science helps them see the rest of life more clearly, they will know that science is important for their students, too.

6

Learning How to Teach Science

While Chapter Five suggested how learning experiences in science could be structured for prospective elementary school teachers, this chapter addresses how these future teachers might best acquire the pedagogical skills and knowledge needed to teach science effectively. The following vignette introduces the connections that prospective teachers should make between their own learning experiences and those of their future students by raising questions for which they must learn together to develop answers.

Renee is a teacher education student who is visiting an elementary classroom as part of her course work in science teaching. The class is studying a demanding concept in science: how nutrients cycle in an ecosystem. Some of the children seem to think that only large animals help cycle nutrients. After all, most know about manure! The children seem to be able to use the terms, but do they really understand the concept of a cycle? Several seem to be confused about how microorganisms contribute to the process. They are having difficulty understanding how nutrients are made available to living organisms by the action of various kinds of decomposers.

Renee begins to ponder the various causes

for the children's difficulty. She reflects on how she learned and began to understand about cycles in ecosystems. What impediments did she have to overcome to master the concept successfully? How can her own experience help her instruct these children? What aspects of their developmental abilities inhibit them from fully grasping the concept? Are children of this age simply unable to fathom such a broad concept? Is the notion of nutrients cycling in an ecosystem just too difficult for them at this age? At what age did she begin to understand cycles? How can she assess whether and how much of the concept the children truly understand? What teaching strategies might she employ for optimum learning? Would a firsthand experience give every child a common basis for discussion? How can she manage this many children in a learning activity?

All the questions Renee is asking herself about the children's learning relate to the art and science of science teaching. Implied in her questions are several very significant notions, including a knowledge of learners and their psychological, emotional, and social characteristics and how these characteristics develop during the elementary school years. What are students capable of doing? What will they want to learn? Also implied is a question of what science is important and appropriate for elementary children to learn. Should children learn vocabulary first and then broad concepts, or vice versa? Matched with this curriculum concern is the question of how Renee will know when a student truly understands a concept, an assessment consideration. Furthermore, she ponders which teaching strategies would be most appropriate for a given science topic. What is the role of firsthand experiences, discussion, and other teaching strategies? Finally, Renee has questions about classroom management. How can she plan and carry out appropriate science learning activities in an organized fashion that allows maximum learning to occur?

The Content of Learning Experiences

Renee's questions and considerations represent a "teachable moment" for her: she is ready to begin to learn much of what is described in Chapter Three as the knowledge, disposition, and skills of an effective elementary school science teacher. What learning experiences can best respond to her needs? We begin to answer this question by considering the content of learning experiences, organized according to the propositions set forth in Chapter Three. In the next section we address how these learning experiences can best be designed.

Commitment to Students and Their Learning

Some of the questions Renee is asking are concerned with what she can expect from children at the age level she is teaching. Preservice teachers need extensive experience with children, investigating their cognitive, social, physical, and emotional development. What interests, abilities, and limitations do children at a certain age exhibit? How do these affect what one can and should teach? Moreover, teachers need to understand the major theories relating to each of these areas. Theories help structure what teachers experience firsthand and provide a common language for discussing particular abilities.

To enrich their exposure to theories of child development, preservice teachers also need programs that continually provide significant practical experience with children from a variety of backgrounds. This will help them apply the theories learned in the college classroom and discern the limits of these theories, as well as begin to understand the range of individual differences they will find in a typical school. One common experience is performing developmental tasks with children of various ages and comparing their responses and abilities. Even more important, prospective teachers need to gain an understanding of how children think about science concepts, as illustrated in the vignette in Chapter Four. Then preservice teachers need help in applying what they have learned about children's thinking to curriculum and instructional methods in science. Without such application, one can expect little transfer of knowledge to the teaching of science.

Of special relevance to this area is the cultural diversity that exists in schools today and the projected increase in diversity over the next decade. According to demographers, the United States will experience a tremendous increase in the number of children from minority groups and children born in poverty in its school population (Hodgkinson, 1985; Spencer, 1989). In some areas of the country, most large urban districts and California, for example, minority students are now in the majority. (A recent newsletter from the Long Beach Unified School District in California reports that its 1992–93 language survey found that at least thirty-seven primary languages were being spoken at home by students in the district.) Preservice teachers need experiences that help them understand the cultural, economic, and social differences they will face in their classrooms; how these differences can affect science learning; and the relationship of these issues to science instruction. Few preservice programs in existence today deal even generally with issues of student diversity as they affect the classroom teacher's job; almost none deal with them specifically in relation to science teaching.

Knowledge of Subject and How to Teach It

Chapter Five describes the kinds of science experiences that help preservice teachers such as Renee feel confident in their understanding of important science concepts and processes. But knowing science and knowing how to teach it are two different things. Many of Renee's questions deal with precisely how to help her students develop an understanding of complicated science concepts.

Much of science teaching involves predicting which concepts students will find difficult, assessing any misconceptions students have about the concepts to be taught, knowing particular sets of science activities that might help students learn certain concepts, anticipating which concepts might require multiple experiences for understanding, and discerning which concepts to avoid with students of a certain age. This kind of teaching knowledge—pedagogical content knowledge—requires an understanding of content and pedagogy and much more. It requires the specific understanding of how particular content matter can best be taught to children of a particular age, that is, what metaphors, strategies, and activities should be used. It also requires an understanding of the social, cultural, and physical conditions that affect the way children in specific elementary school classes will approach learning in general and the content in question in particular (Cochran, King, and De-Ruiter, in press).

One of the primary missions of preservice elementary programs is to provide experiences that will allow preservice teachers to acquire pedagogical content knowledge in science. The following vignette serves as an illustration.

Angelle and Joseph, two teacher education students, work three afternoons a week in a first-grade classroom. They and their classmates are paired up in teams so that they can observe each other and discuss their work together. Both Angelle and Joseph had assumed that they would teach primary grades, and now they are learning that there is a lot more than they had realized to working with very young children.

Even though Ms. McClain is an experienced first-grade teacher, she has never felt that she has done anything very interesting in science, so she is delighted to have Angelle and Joseph in her classroom. Ms. McClain is finding that, while she is helping these teacher education students learn, she is learning from them as well.

Today Joseph will begin an exploration of the water cycle with the class. This idea occurred to both Angelle and Joseph because so many of the children are curious about where rain comes from. They discovered that the children already have many theories about it. Some think that rain comes from the sky, kind of like the shower in the bathtub at home. Others think that rain comes out of the air because that's

*where they feel it. Still others think that rain comes
from snow that is up in heaven and melts and falls
down. Angelle will run the camcorder today; she and
Joseph take turns at this.*

*Joseph calls the children to the rug at the
back of the room and begins: "Many of you have
been talking about where the rain comes from. Today we are going to begin working to see if we can
figure that out."*

"Are we going to do an esperment?*" asks
one little girl. The children have been enjoying the
kinds of things that Angelle and Joseph have been
doing with them.*

"What could we do?" asks Joseph.

*"We could put a container out and see next
time it rains where it is coming from," suggests one
of the boys.*

*"What do you mean? It is raining right now!"
exclaims another child.*

*Joseph suggests that they see what kinds of
ideas they already have about where the rain
comes from. "What are some of your* hypotheses?*"
he asks.*

*Several children are eager to tell what they
think, and Joseph carefully writes their ideas down
on a large sheet of paper.*

*After recording several ideas, Joseph lets the
children put some containers outside in the rain and
suggests that over the next few days they watch to
see if there is more rain and what happens to the
rain that is in the containers.*

"It will dry up!*" call out several children.*

"But how?*" asks one of the girls.*

*After the children set their containers outside
and return to the classroom, Joseph asks them to*

*draw a picture or write something in their science
notebooks that shows what they think will happen
to the containers.*

Angelle and Joseph are building their understanding of how first graders think about rain; subsequently, the two will learn how to help their students learn more.

Listed below are some examples of pedagogical content knowledge related to teaching about another topic—in this case, plants. Notice that some examples relate to students' misconceptions, others relate to knowledge of what learners can master at a particular age, and still others relate to understanding how students best learn particular concepts.

Knowledge About Children's Concept Development
- Students often confuse plant food with food that animals eat (Roth, 1989).
- Photosynthesis is exceedingly complicated. Most elementary students will only understand the general notion that it is a process by which most plants make their own food and that this process requires sunlight and a gas called carbon dioxide. The end result of photosynthesis is the creation of sugar.
- When experimenting with plants, many children believe that if a plant grows tall, even if the plant is weak and spindly, it is healthier than one that is short, strong, and bushy.
- Truly understanding concepts that deal with atoms and molecules (for example, the chemical and energy processes involved in photosynthesis) is difficult for elementary children because they cannot see, feel, hear, or otherwise experience particles this small.

Knowledge About Teaching Strategies
- Giving students many opportunities to experiment with various planting and growing conditions will establish a base of firsthand experience about plants upon which they can build in later years.
- For younger elementary children, using microscopes to look at leaves can be counterproductive because they do not under-

stand what they are looking at. Hand-held magnifiers are easier for them to manipulate, and they understand what they see.

• It is important to have students relate their classroom experience with plants to their home experience with them. What parts of plants do they eat? How can they create a productive vegetable garden? What plants do they see in their yard, on the playground, or in the forest? What uses besides food are made of particular plants?

• Because of its complexity, teaching about photosynthesis is best left until the end of the elementary years or the beginning of the middle grades.

Curriculum Knowledge

• Curriculum materials developed by the Elementary Science Study (ESS, published by Delta) contain many excellent activities that can help elementary students learn about plants. Important units include *The Life of Beans and Peas, Growing Seeds,* and *Budding Twigs.* (Other relevant curriculum materials are noted later in this chapter.)

Similar analyses can be done for other science topics in the typical elementary science curriculum, for example, energy, heat, magnetism, electricity, human body functions and systems, weather, rocks and minerals, ecology, and so on. Additional analyses can be done by the preservice teachers. Experiences that allow preservice teacher education students to understand how best to teach these topics can also be designed.

Managing and Monitoring Student Learning

Renee is ready for learning experiences in the area of managing and monitoring student learning. This includes determining goals for science learning, selecting appropriate topics and teaching materials, developing a repertoire of instructional strategies, and using a variety of assessment methods.

Choosing Goals. Preservice elementary teachers need to spend time analyzing and discussing the goals of elementary science education. Only from an understanding of issues related to this question can they seek answers to more practical questions, such as how elementary science should be taught. One set of broad goals for elementary science curriculum and instruction comes from the National Center for Improving Science Education's (1989) elementary report series:

- To develop children's innate curiosity about the world
- To broaden children's procedural and thinking skills for investigating the world, solving problems, and making decisions
- To increase children's knowledge of the natural world
- To develop children's understanding of the nature of science and technology
- To develop children's understanding of the limits and possibilities of science and technology

The report series also identifies broad concepts, attitudes, and skills that compose a framework for teaching elementary school science (Bybee and others, 1989). These outcomes, listed in Table 6.1, are parallel to those stressed in Chapters Three and Five as required for teachers themselves. (Adaptations are made—for example, with respect to the broad concepts or themes—and some con-

Table 6.1. Broad Concepts, Attitudes, and Skills for Teaching Elementary School Science.

Broad Concepts		
Organization	Cause and effect	Systems
Scale	Models	Change
Structure and function	Variation	Diversity
Scientific Attitudes		
Desiring knowledge	Being skeptical	Relying on data
Accepting ambiguity	Being willing to mod-	Cooperating
Respecting reason	ify explanation	Being honest
Inquiry Skills		
Observing	Making inferences	Classifying
Measuring	Making predictions	Experimenting
Building models	Practical lab skills	

Source: Adapted from National Center for Improving Science Education, 1989.

cepts listed in Chapter Five are divided into several simpler ones appropriate for the lower grades.)

Reading and discussing publications that deal with the goals and curricular and instructional outcomes in elementary school science is a useful way for preservice teachers to begin to address significant curriculum issues and controversies about the goals of elementary science education. Doing this will introduce preservice teachers to the fact that they may have to face significant national and local differences concerning goals, outcomes, and curricular choices once they are in the classroom.

After general goals and outcomes are clarified, there arises the question, What science topics should an elementary teacher teach her or his students (although in situations such as Renee's, someone else has already made this decision)? Preservice teachers need experience in selecting topics that not only appeal to children of a particular age but also incorporate the broad organizing concepts important in elementary science. Moreover, they need experience in developing topics of study that will help students develop their inquiry skills (Black, 1987). Typical topics that provide these opportunities are plants, rocks and minerals, and life cycles. All three topics incorporate a variety of organizing concepts and inquiry skills. For example, the topic of plants can illustrate the broad concept of systems (if the unit focuses on plant systems) or structure and function (if the unit stresses plant parts and functions). Likewise, a unit on life cycles might emphasize the broad concept of diversity (if the emphasis is on the life cycles of many different organisms) or change (if the notion of cycle is stressed).

Choosing Curriculum Materials. Elementary teachers rarely have the time, resources, or expertise to create lessons for each topic they teach. Therefore, preservice teachers need opportunities to learn about the many curriculum materials for elementary school science that already exist. These include units and lessons used over the last twenty years such as those from the *Elementary Science Study* (ESS) and from the *Science Curriculum Improvement Study* (SCIS). They also include more recently developed units that stress both broad organizing concepts and inquiry skills, such as those from *Insights* (developed by Education Development Corporation), *Science for*

Life and Living (developed by Biological Sciences Curriculum Study—BSCS), and *Science and Technology for Children* (developed by the National Science Resources Center). Other examples of newer materials are the *Great Exploration in Math and Science* (GEMS) and the *Full Option Science System* (FOSS), both developed by the Lawrence Hall of Science. BSCS has undertaken a project called Teacher Development Modules that will analyze the main features of several of these new curriculum materials and provide extensive classroom footage dealing with curriculum, instruction and learning, and assessment.

Many elementary science curriculum materials in circulation are not well conceived and do not stress the concepts and skills important to teach at this level. Preservice teachers need opportunities to analyze and critique an assortment of science curriculum resources. By reviewing both superior and inferior examples, they can begin to develop a method for distinguishing and making choices among materials, as the following vignette illustrates.

Dr. Rossin's teacher education students are analyzing and comparing several units that were developed to help elementary school children explore how plants make food (laying the base for later, more rigorous study of photosynthesis). He has gathered units from several popular text series as well as a few investigations developed outside of textbooks.

Dr. Rossin thinks that the teacher education students in his course are well prepared to appraise the different approaches to teaching this topic. They have dealt with photosynthesis as learners themselves. In fact, there were some major arguments during that segment of the course! They have also observed children of different ages exploring the way plants make food.

Some of the teacher education students have seen videotapes of interviews with children. Others have worked with multimedia materials from a fourth-grade classroom, including videotapes of several lessons on photosynthesis and copies of students' written work on the topic. The students spent several class sessions comparing notes on what they saw and heard in those materials, which helped them understand more about what children think.

Now, as the students analyze the strengths and weaknesses of the various units Dr. Rossin has provided, they are considering what they understand about the scientific topic as well as what they know about children's understanding of it.

Dr. Rossin has used this approach before, although the use of multimedia materials is new this year. In the past, he had his students observe a couple of local teachers teaching this topic. He suspects that this year's students may have gotten a deeper understanding of how children think, but he is not sure. The multimedia materials have allowed the students to look very closely at a particular child's comments during class and then to trace the same child's thinking in the written work. This seems promising because the action in classrooms being observed is sometimes so fast that observers cannot always probe deeply enough into what is happening.

Dr. Rossin's aim is to help his students further develop their understanding of photosynthesis as well as to integrate their ideas about young students and about how to deal with the very real pedagogical challenge of finding good instructional materials. He hopes that this project will help the prospective teachers be better prepared to do the same thing with other topics.

As Dr. Rossin observes the prospective

*teachers discussing the materials in their groups, he
makes some notes, for he wants to have a preliminary conversation about the project in class tomorrow. Overhearing one student's comment that the
materials he is reviewing would merely support
children's common idea that plant food is what
nourishes plants, Dr. Rossin asks the student to be
prepared to talk about his concern in class tomorrow and to point out specific things in the materials
that are causing that concern.*

As noted in Chapter One, science textbooks play a significant
role in elementary science education. Many critics believe that this
role is detrimental because the best-selling series tend to stress an
encyclopedic study of science, overemphasize the recall of facts and
terms, and incorporate only a superficial emphasis on scientific
inquiry. Other science educators believe that a well-written textbook can provide a structure from which the elementary teacher can
teach science, which they consider preferable to encouraging individual elementary teachers to develop their own curricula.

Given that any text will have both good and bad features,
preservice elementary teachers need to become wary and critical
consumers of the various text series on the market. What are the
characteristics of a well-written series? Can the shortcomings of one
textbook be easily offset by the use of an activity supplement? Can
the application of particular teaching strategies make the text series
more appropriate to the needs of elementary children and the goals
of elementary science? Teacher education programs must give preservice students an opportunity to devise methods for analyzing and
critiquing textbooks and answering questions such as these.

Choosing Teaching Strategies. Many of Renee's questions focus on
how to teach, or what teaching strategies to use. Teaching strategies
are ways of organizing lessons or learning events to optimize student understanding. Many strategies are common to teaching almost any topic or subject, including discussion, questioning,
demonstration, lab activity, finding and using existing sources of

knowledge (including the textbook), and appropriate lecture techniques. Preservice teachers need opportunities to practice each of these strategies on numerous occasions. They must become expert at using the strategies to conduct lessons and expert at deciding when to use each of the strategies, an ability they will continue to develop after they begin teaching.

Two strategies and one aspect of most lessons are so important to the teaching and learning of science that they bear special mention. The first strategy is cooperative learning, in which students work together in groups to accomplish specific learning goals (Johnson, Johnson, Holubec, and Roy, 1984). Children typically are assigned specific roles (recorder, team leader, materials manager), which are rotated so that students experience a full range of responsibility over a period of time. Moreover, the teacher structures the task to ensure that individuals depend on each other to achieve results. Preservice teachers need abundant opportunities to practice using the principles of cooperative learning in planning and carrying out science lessons. An excellent learning strategy is to have the preservice teachers experience cooperative learning themselves in both content and methods courses. Later, they will have to learn how to set up groups and assign roles, keep their students on task, and structure group work without dominating it.

A second strategy critical to teaching science is carrying out a hands-on activity. So much emphasis is placed on firsthand experience in science that providing opportunities for elementary students to interact with materials and gain this experience is central to the role of science teaching. Yet carrying out such an activity is not as easy as it appears. Teachers must decide how to organize the activity to provide maximum learning within a relatively short period of time. They must select the activity, find appropriate materials, decide how the materials will be distributed, ensure that students actually work on the intended tasks, collect the materials, provide opportunities for students to share what they have learned, and help students create new understandings with their classmates. By having several opportunities to observe and then practice the implementation of hands-on activities, preservice teachers will begin to internalize and actually become accomplished in this complex cycle of events. To carry out such activities successfully, prospective teachers need considerable experience in managing materials. They must accustom themselves to organizing, distributing, and maintaining materials by beginning to do these things in their preservice content and methods courses and by discussing how best to accomplish the tasks.

Especially critical to learning from a science lesson is giving students an opportunity to make sense of what they have experienced. Without a well-organized session in which students are asked to summarize what they have experienced and relate their experiences to the concepts they already understand, a hands-on activity becomes simply time to "play" with science materials; the well-meant demonstration becomes only an entertaining show. Discussion sessions among students also allow the teacher to assess how well students have understood the activity. Students may successfully complete a hands-on activity without connecting it to the concept behind it (Fosnot, 1989). Yet this extremely important "minds-on" component of a science activity is easily overlooked, perhaps because it is one of the most difficult aspects of science teaching for new teachers to carry out properly. To be effective, elementary school teachers must help students make sense of what they know and what they have experienced. Most preservice teachers need multiple opportunities to practice this rounding out of a lesson and reflection on their practice. As John R. Baird, Peter J. Fensham, Richard F. Gunstone, and Richard T. White (1991) have shown, students reflect on their learning only when their teachers also reflect on the learning they expect from a lesson or instructional sequence.

Choosing Assessment Methods. Renee also asks several questions about assessment, which in the last several years has occupied a central role in American schools. Most teachers use assessment primarily for accountability. Scores must be assigned, grades must be given, and reports must be filed for all students. The problem with this use of assessment is that it focuses learning on the things that are easily measured, usually the recall of simple facts. Wanting students to do well on such assessments, teachers and other school officials have shaped the nature of instruction so that definitions of terms, verbal explanations, and labels for concepts have become the focus of much science teaching.

Recently, an expanded understanding of the place of assessment in science teaching—one that stresses the integral role of assessment in the teaching and learning process—has emerged. Since many concepts are built upon pre- or corequisite concepts, ensuring that students have learned previous material is a necessary step in the teaching/learning process. Such assessment (often labeled "authentic") does the following:

- Matches instruction and is indistinguishable from instructional tasks
- Includes hands-on performance tasks
- Probes the child's depth of understanding
- Includes an array of informal techniques, including systems by which teachers record their observations of students, document student performances, and evaluate student understanding
- Includes children's assessment of their own work, so they can begin to reflect about their progress and growth in science knowledge and thinking [National Center for Improving Science Education, 1989, p. 28].

Preservice teachers need opportunities to discuss, develop, and try out various kinds of assessment that have these characteristics. They should begin to see that instruction and assessment are two sides of the same coin, two parts of the same whole that focuses on student learning of important concepts in science and on science as a way of knowing.

Thinking About Teaching and Learning from Experience

Renee's questions are a prime example of the kinds of questions teachers constantly ought to ask about their practice. One of the goals of any teacher education program should be to help Renee and her peers learn how to be more systematic about asking questions and pursuing good answers to them.

Underlying the development of the kind of elementary school teachers of science we envision is the notion of educating teachers who reflect on the practice of teaching (Calderhead, 1992), teachers who think about their teaching and the decisions they make before, during, and after instruction. No matter what skills, understanding, or knowledge they acquire through various preservice teacher education experiences, developing teachers must, above all, be able to think about the many situations they encounter in science teaching and be willing to attempt innovative solutions to problems that arise. By reflecting on their experiences, elementary school teachers learn to think on their feet, diagnose student difficulties, apply potential learning solutions, and evaluate whether the prescribed solutions have had the desired outcome. The reflective practitioner is one who inquires about teaching, reflects on what students do or do not know, collects data on what students understand, and makes decisions on the basis of the data rather than what he or she abstractly thinks is appropriate (Fosnot, 1989). Finally, such a teacher considers the "hidden" social lessons (related to race, class, and gender) being conveyed by materials, activities, and interactions and then addresses them as necessary.

It is unlikely that new teachers can emerge from preservice programs fully able to solve all of the teaching and learning problems they will face. However, they must have the skills, confidence, and disposition to engage in the process of problem solving. Thus, preservice teachers must be exposed to a teacher education program that treats teaching as a problem-solving activity. They must have multiple opportunities to work with children and to analyze and study the effects of their efforts with them. They must have opportunities to discuss and deliberate about their own teaching and that of others, with their peers, experienced classroom teachers, and professors. They must, in short, begin to reflect on the practice of teaching, especially their own teaching (Schön, 1987), a habit they will reenforce throughout their teaching career.

Teachers as Members of Learning Communities

Renee's questions focus on the immediate classroom; her teacher education program needs to help her resolve her concerns about how best to teach important science concepts to children. More importantly, it must also help her see beyond the classroom, both in terms of how to bring the outside world into her classroom and in terms of how to contribute to the strength of her school and district through collaborative activities.

Learning activities for preservice teachers need to include the use of community resources to promote learning. Science lends itself well to this because there is a wide range of possible resources upon which to draw. Among these are local science and engineering laboratories and businesses, public agencies concerned with health and the environment, zoos, parks, and science museums. Parents— both those with some science expertise and/or science careers and those interested in learning along with their children—are also rich sources of support. Preservice teachers should learn about the Association of Science and Technology Centers (ASTC), which networks such informal science organizations as zoos, museums, and aquariums. They can use materials from *Family Science* (Northwest Equals Program, in press) to engage parents in their children's science learning. Preservice teachers should be encouraged, in all their development activities, to include resources available outside the classroom.

Being part of the learning community called the school is a very important aspect of teaching. It is especially important for elementary teachers interested in and committed to science because science often does not receive substantive attention at that level. Research indicates that schools where teachers work together on a regular basis, constantly building new approaches to meet their children's needs, are schools in which children learn more (Little, 1982). Prospective teachers can be prepared for this role of collaborator by working on learning teams (after careful preparation) throughout their preservice program and by being part of school teams in all their field experiences.

It is not clear, however, that during the preservice program is the time to focus heavily on preparing prospective teachers for responsible roles in curriculum, policy, and staff development because only so much can be included in a program (especially one that espouses a "depth versus breadth" approach). Perhaps exposure to the possibilities of such roles through some minimal reading, as well as through working on teams in the schools to which they are assigned, is sufficient for this first phase of their development as teachers.

Social, Ethical, and Civic Implications

Science is a content area fraught with value judgments, especially when applications to the real world are attempted. What does it mean to save endangered species, clean up pollution, and save the forests when doing so threatens someone's livelihood? What are the issues surrounding scientific investigation and experimentation when professional reputations and a corporation's profits and losses are at stake? Preservice teachers need opportunities to consider such issues when they themselves are doing science or designing science learning experiences for children.

The scientific habits of mind that have become legitimate outcomes of school science (see Chapter Five) are relevant here as well. Helping preservice teachers develop ways of encouraging honesty, skepticism, and patience in their and their students' science work is important, as is developing ways of assessing whether their students do, in fact, have these attitudes. Similarly, preservice teachers need exposure to issues of equity—gender, cultural, racial, and so on—as they work with students and design learning experiences. A program such as *Teacher Expectations and Student Achievement* (TESA) (Kerman, 1979) or *Gender/Ethnic Expectations and Student Achievement* (GESA) (Grayson and Martin, 1988) can help prospective teachers see how their interactions with students are influenced by their expectations for the students' success, as well as the extent to which their interactions with students provide more opportunities for some to learn than others. These are issues that teachers need to address across the content areas, but they are especially salient in science, for several population groups are underrepresented in science careers, in large part because of the way they are treated in school.

The Nature and Design of Learning Experiences

What we believe preservice teachers should learn is but one part of the story, for *how* that learning is accomplished is at least as important. If new teachers are to use an inquiry-based, constructivist approach in their teaching, for example, then it is critical that their own learning experiences be designed in that way. In this section we consider eight "design specifications" or characteristics of effective learning experiences for preservice teachers of science:

1. Learning experiences are designed to help preservice teachers "construct" their own knowledge about learning and teaching.
2. Learning experiences provide multiple structured opportunities for interaction and communication between preservice students.
3. Learning experiences model multiple paths for learning.
4. Learning experiences unfold over time.
5. Learning experiences provide opportunities to create and synthesize knowledge.
6. Learning experiences include opportunities for reflection and self-correction.
7. Learning experiences incorporate opportunities to practice the craft of teaching in real and simulated situations.
8. Learning experiences reflect the values of patience, diversity, honesty, skepticism, and risk taking.

This list illustrates the parallelism we wish to reflect in this book: the same features that apply to preservice teachers' learning of science ought to characterize the learning experiences they design for their students.

Teachers "Constructing" Knowledge

In our depiction of an ideal classroom in Chapters Two and Four, we describe the value of a generative learning model that supports the construction of knowledge by the learner. Different from the one-way delivery of new information, this and similar models engage learners in a way that relates to their current knowledge and experiences; provide opportunities for exploration and experimentation; propose explanations for the phenomena of interest, that is, the scientific or pedagogical principles at work; and provide opportunities for application to different situations. The steps inherent in such models help learners articulate, challenge, and build on their own conceptions, leading to richer and more complex understanding.

Figure 4.1 illustrates a learning experience that was designed according to such a model. Depending on the desired learning outcome, all steps of the model may not be appropriate; neither may the given sequence always be the best one. There still is a great difference, however, between learning experiences designed with this kind of model in mind and the lecture/discussion or lecture/confirmatory-lab designs prevalent in college classrooms. Allen A. Black and Paul P. Ammon (1992) demonstrated that students entering a graduate certification program initially favored a traditional teaching approach—no doubt reflecting their own undergraduate experience—but after exposure to a constructivist teacher education program, they favored more constructivist approaches. Furthermore, Black and Ammon report, many of the program graduates adopted these approaches in their own teaching, suggesting that the pedagogical approach of the teacher education program can play a major role in changing students' views and practices.

Here are some strategies for incorporating constructivist approaches into learning experiences for preservice teachers:

- At the beginning of a learning activity, have preservice students depict or discuss their current conceptions of the topic under examination.
- Provide structured opportunities for preservice teachers to observe or work with children, and debrief the experience before discussing or presenting new material.
- For such difficult concepts as constructivism, provide multiple opportunities for preservice teachers to investigate, observe, experiment, and so forth.
- Carefully develop ways for preservice teachers to apply their new knowledge to new situations.
- Ask preservice teachers to keep journals as they develop their knowledge about teaching.

Multiple Structured Opportunities for Interaction

Future teachers typically have experienced learning as a solitary proposition in which competition with peers and independent achievement are valued. Yet current conceptions of learning point toward a very different scenario. Learning is seen as occurring quite often through social interaction (Vygotsky, 1986; Johnson, Johnson, Holubec, and Roy, 1984; American Psychological Association, 1991). Although people may discover an insight or come to understand an idea in a new way on their own, it is usually through discussing it, presenting it—in short, "bouncing it off" respected peers—that they come to refine and solidify their understanding. Through such dialogue, they construct new meanings and begin to consider different perspectives. Preservice teachers learn better when their learning experiences promote dialogue and collaboration.

Another reason for collegial structures in teacher preparation relates to current changes occurring in schools. More than ever before, today's schools require teachers to participate in a variety of collaborative structures. In some states, for example, school improvement legislation mandates that teachers work on teams with parents and other educators to chart the future of the school. The interdisciplinary curriculum of many middle schools requires teachers to work together to design and implement units for students they team teach. Finally, improvement of one's own teaching necessitates interaction with one or more trusted and respected colleagues—one of the greatest sources of professional knowledge. In short, being a teacher is no longer a close-your-door proposition.

Because of the natural desire to learn through social interaction and the collaborative nature of today's schools, it is imperative for teacher preparation experiences to build in opportunities for professional interaction. We suggest any or all of the following strategies for doing this:

- Use cohort groups in which a number of prospective teachers move through a program together to encourage and build interaction and support within and outside courses.
- Team teach to show interrelationships between content, methods, and other courses.
- Use various room arrangements—not in rows but in clusters, horseshoes, and other interaction-enhancing configurations.
- Use cooperative learning strategies (Johnson, Johnson, Holubec, and Roy, 1984): jigsaw (small groups of students investi-

gating different parts of a question, then all groups pooling information), teams in games and tournaments, student-team learning, study groups, and so forth.

- Assign group projects and presentations.
- Incorporate team-building, communication, and trust-building activities.
- Model substantive interaction between faculty members (sometimes including students) during departmental seminars, symposia, demonstrations of "master classes," analyses of cases, and so forth.
- Provide clinical experiences for clusters of preservice teachers, with regular seminars to share, analyze, and reflect upon experiences.

Multiple Paths for Learning

Not all human beings learn best through the same activity or approach (Guild and Garger, 1985). Some like to hear things, others need to see them, and still others must be able to handle concrete objects manually to gain understanding. Some people like to order things sequentially; others prefer more random arrangements. One person likes bright light and silence for studying; another requires soft light and background music. Some learners need to see the big picture first and then the details; others cannot understand the big picture until they grasp the details. The variations go on and on.

Our purpose here is not to synthesize the research on learning styles, modes, and preferences. It is merely to call attention to the fact that, while learners display a large variety of learning preferences and needs, most individuals tend to teach in the ways that they learn best. This poses a fundamental challenge to teacher educators to provide multiple paths for learning *and* to engage future teachers in an analysis of their own preferred learning styles. By providing multiple ways of learning, teacher educators can model what they hope future teachers will do. By engaging teacher education students in self-analysis, they help develop a willingness and ability to appeal to the styles of all learners.

Does this mean that teacher educators should strive to individualize programs to fit each future teacher's style? We certainly do not expect this. Preservice teachers should be encouraged to learn in ways that best suit them, but they also need learning experiences that help them practice other styles. If prospective teachers are to learn to teach toward other learning modes, they must experience what it feels like to learn in those modes. Thus, we encourage stretching future teachers into modes of learning other than their own.

Here are several strategies for incorporating multiple paths of learning into learning experiences for preservice teachers:

- Use activities and assignments that help students learn through a variety of modes; make these modes explicit and label them.
- Compare and contrast multiple approaches to teaching the same topic in terms of the learning styles that are embedded in each approach.
- Try out and discuss various models of problem solving—for example, "forest" as contrasted with "trees," "planned" as contrasted with "serendipitous," "I'll need some help" as contrasted with "I'll solve it myself," "innovative" as contrasted with "step-by-step." Discuss how these relate to various learning styles, modes, and preferences.
- Use several ways of evaluating the course work and clinical experiences of teacher education students.
- Allow options for individual work or group work for projects, observations, and so on.
- Allow assignments to be done in a variety of ways: poster, video, written paper, oral report.
- Include self-assessment of learning styles through sharing among those with the same style (How do we learn best? Then how are we likely to teach? How can we push ourselves to teach in styles different from our own?).
- Have students present material in a style different from their preferred mode (in microteaching or during clinical experiences).

Learning over Time

By urging that learning continue over time, we intend that there be systematic, planned experiences that build toward skill, insight, and deep conceptualization of what it means to be a teacher. This follows from the proposition that complex ideas and behavior changes are not developed overnight. The mastery of important concepts or approaches is facilitated in a spiraling manner, with many opportunities to meet an idea in a variety of contexts. A formidable challenge today, as we have emphasized, is educating children from all cultures and backgrounds. Rather than requiring a course in multicultural education, this challenge ought to be a theme or strand common to a variety of courses and field experiences. Other important concepts (with their accompanying skills and strategies) to be met continuously and developed during the program are described in earlier sections: the constructivist view of learning, variations in learning styles, collaborative learning, societal and ethical concerns, and so on. Primary among these themes or strands is pedagogical content knowledge in science, with its accompanying set of understandings and strategies, which needs to be consciously developed over time.

Another perspective on this "over time" issue relates to how science is done by scientists. Scientific investigation is not a quick endeavor; usually, it is a long, drawn-out activity, sometimes with no end in sight. Rather than conceiving of their own learning as occurring in chunks of instructional periods or semesters, future teachers need to realize that their growth and that of their students will develop progressively over time. One way to build this awareness is to engage teacher education students in long-term projects. An example is a year-long project studying how children develop their understanding of seasonal water flow in a stream and how this relates to rain or runoff. Such a "long view" might stimulate careful observation and appreciation of the scientific process as well as the learning process, both in the teacher-learners and in their student-learners.

Strategies that can be used to incorporate the concept of learning over time include the following:

- Refer back to and build on previously discussed issues to help students develop new understandings and synthesize new ideas.
- Reiterate a concept or principle over the period of a semester or year; design or point out multiple experiences or illustrations in

a variety of settings so that preservice teachers can truly recognize the concept when they encounter it.

- Revisit concepts of teaching and learning by using several different approaches; see them in action, read and discuss or debate them, try them out, and so forth.
- Use progressive, sequential, continuous reflection.
- Have students keep portfolios to remind themselves of previous activities.
- Emphasize real problems that occur repeatedly over time.
- Use major learning activities and projects that require many steps for a comprehensive analysis of an issue.

Opportunities to Create and Synthesize

Courses and clinical experiences need to engage future teachers in higher-level thinking, not just memorization and rote imitation. In such a view of instruction, the students are active constructors of knowledge rather than absorbers of someone else's (the professor's) "right" answers. Further, they are able to integrate their learning; they do not see one course's content as separate from that of another course when they consider the act of teaching. In reality, all professional knowledge gained through courses and field activities is considered together when responding to a teaching challenge, whether it be a debate around a hypothetical situation, a practical lesson or activity, or a response to a dilemma encountered in practice teaching.

This kind of synthesis does not happen through osmosis; it requires explicit guidance and modeling. Teacher educators need to develop in preservice teachers an understanding of what it means to synthesize; often, these students think synthesis is summary and become fearful or feel limited when asked to synthesize what they have learned. They need to practice and explore such higher-level thinking. From teacher educators, they need clear models, guidelines, and assignments that challenge them to create both technical products (for example, lessons) *and* critical arguments about educational dilemmas (for example, mainstreaming/inclusion, ways of knowing, equity issues, core curriculum).

Here are some possible strategies for incorporating such

higher-level thinking into learning experiences for preservice teachers:

- Analyze video episodes or cases that demonstrate a variety of perspectives, social issues, psychological issues, technical methods (Harrington and Garrison, 1992).
- Create course blocks with teams of professors teaching a cohort group of preservice teachers, with an emphasis on the common ideas in the courses and assignments that require analysis from multiple perspectives (for example, across such courses as Social Foundations of Education, Curriculum and Methods, and Measurement and Evaluation).
- Include debates, discussion, and analysis of cases using a variety of perspectives and information.
- Design assessments related to a particular approach to teaching a given topic; debate the pros and cons of each approach in terms of the assessment called for.

Opportunities for Reflection and Self-Correction

The ultimate goal is to develop autonomous teachers who can actively inquire into their teaching and their students' learning. As already noted, such inquiry and continuous learning require reflection and self-correction. How does such a process occur? According to Amy B. Colton and Georgea Sparks-Langer (1993), there are two aspects to consider: the first is the professional knowledge the teacher must call upon when making a teaching decision—knowledge about content, students, methods, context, prior experience, and personal beliefs; the second is the process of reflective thinking, which can be described through the model of experiential learning (Kolb, 1984).

Upon encountering an opportunity for a decision, a teacher either activates an automatic script that was learned previously (for example, stand near a student whose attention is wandering) or begins to reflect consciously on the situation. After observing the situation (for example, a student looking confused about how to connect wires to a battery and bulbs), the teacher usually will begin to analyze the event by accessing and evaluating relevant information (for example, this child may have a hearing problem; I'd better check the records). As the teacher continues to reflect upon the situation, other sources of information may become relevant. As a result of considering another viewpoint or new information, the teacher may reframe the problem and choose a different path of action (for example, this child may have been warned against touching anything electric; I'd better bring in a lamp and let her replace the lightbulb or discuss an example she is familiar with). Such reframing and consideration of several perspectives on an event are at the heart of reflective thought.

Well-designed teacher education experiences develop the habits of reflective decision making—in short, metacognitive "scripts" for self-questioning that prompt the examination of a variety of points of view and information sources. Such reflection occurs before one chooses an action, during the act of teaching, or when inquiring into the results of one's practice.

The reflective thought we are proposing is not unidimensional—it occurs on at least two levels: (1) the technical (or micro) level of reflection tends to be functional, short term, a rather "what works" pragmatism; (2) the critical (or macro) level of reflection encompasses questions of ethics, justice, and caring (Van Maanen, 1977). Beginning teachers function at the micro, or technical, level when considering which classroom rule will successfully get students to come in from recess and get right to work. Teachers only move to the macro, or critical, level when they begin to ask themselves what that rule will be teaching children in terms of living in a democratic society. They might ask themselves, If all classroom rules are to be obeyed and never discussed or questioned, is this a desirable habit to develop in these children?

We propose the following strategies for developing reflective thinking:

- Provide preservice teachers with opportunities and requirements for the analysis of their own and others' teaching and learning episodes.
- Link pedagogy and science courses together conceptually so that future teachers begin to access knowledge from both domains when analyzing the learning of students.

- Use peer or partner reflection as a way of processing a lesson, unit, or performance (as in scientific investigations).
- Use microteaching in real or simulated situations, and then, after self-reflection and revision, teach the revised lesson.
- Assign journals in which preservice teachers guide their self-questioning before and after teaching and develop lists of questions they need to ask themselves (modeling, prompting, and guiding metacognition).
- Have preservice teachers analyze a written case of teaching or learning at both the technical and critical levels.
- Through readings, discussions, and writing, prompt students to analyze their own entering conceptions of teaching, learning, and science ideas in terms of the kind of learner they are and the kinds of learners they will teach.
- Provide opportunities for preservice teachers to take on multiple perspectives—cultural, gender, social background—through the analysis of cases, content, and episodes that are culturally or socially outside their own life experiences.
- Have preservice teachers analyze their own development of a key concept, such as classification, as a course progresses; have them analyze their own visualization of the concept and link their development process to that of a child.
- During a microteaching lesson on a common science topic, have both the "teacher" and the "learners" assess their own understanding of the ideas as a result of the questions that were asked about the underlying concepts during the lesson.

Opportunities to Practice

The word *practice,* as used here, has two meanings. First, it means repeating an activity, construction, or performance several times to enable oneself to reflect upon it and thereby improve. Teaching is very complicated; mastery does not occur quickly. While the mechanics can often be observed quite easily in simulated situations, the process becomes much more complex when one is working with a class of twenty-five to thirty children. Juggling all the aspects of teaching in an elementary classroom requires the wisdom that comes with numerous experiences combined with self-assessment and feedback from another person.

The second meaning of the word *practice* complements the first. It means doing something in a real-world setting—moving off campus to the elementary school classroom and community, where learning and teaching occur, and actively trying out new behaviors and skills. In short, preservice teachers need to experience observing, analyzing, and teaching in several contexts. They need to assume gradually all the responsibilities of teachers. This probably will require practicing separately some or all of the skills, and strategies discussed earlier in this chapter before practicing them in combination. Eventually, however, prospective teachers need to work with real learners in real settings. They need to work in a variety of cultural and educational settings. And they need to immerse themselves not only in the generic skills of teaching but also in the analysis of content and the dilemmas of schooling.

How might this be accomplished? The following strategies are recommended:

- Use a sequence of pedagogical learning settings that begins with classroom observations and progresses to work with one child, then with small groups, then with an entire class. Build in reflection time between the experiences to allow for discussion of how the approach needs to change as more children are included.
- Have students design, teach, redesign, and reteach several lessons or units involving a cross section of age levels and science learning outcomes.
- Have students analyze resources and science topics to find main themes, important concepts, and thinking skills that might be developed.
- Have students collect and analyze a variety of materials that teach a particular topic; for example, how do ESS, SCIS, GEMS, Macmillan, and Heath present and develop the concept of sound? Students should isolate the principles and curricular structure of each approach.
- Have students analyze several videos of teaching and learning

episodes by using the ideas they have learned to interpret the events observed.

- Into all development and practice teaching experiences, build reflection activities that include identification of what to change in the next similar opportunity.
- Have a cohort of preservice teachers discuss their lessons. Interject materials they have developed as well as videos of their teaching episodes; require regular reflection on their learning over time, observed changes, and so forth.
- Have prospective teachers develop and try out several kinds of assessment of individual students' conceptual understanding of particular science topics.
- Working in suburban, rural, and inner-city schools, have individual preservice teachers develop a relationship with a child and/or family different from their own; have them maintain and examine the experience over time.

Reflecting the Values of Patience, Diversity, Honesty, Skepticism, and Risk Taking

Throughout this book, we mention the importance of developing in both students and teachers "scientific habits of mind." These attitudes, it turns out, are useful far beyond the pursuit of scientific understanding and should characterize preservice teacher education experiences as well.

Learning is not a matter of antiseptic, "objective," value-free facts and knowledge. Teaching and learning involve relationships between people; and wherever such relationships exist, values and ethics enter in. Therefore, designers of learning experiences for preservice teachers need to consider carefully the values they model and promote both implicitly and explicitly. For example, learning experiences that take place only in settings that lack minorities may not be modeling the value of diversity that the designers hope to develop in preservice teachers.

One obvious place to start developing those values is with those who "deliver" the learning experiences: professors and mentor teachers. These are the models to whom the aspiring teacher looks for socially acceptable norms of behavior. Are they patient, considerate, and caring? Do they demonstrate honesty? Do they have an inquiring mind? Do they take risks, and are they skeptical of surface appearances? Models are always more powerful when they are labeled, discussed, and analyzed by the learners. Such analysis can be encouraged in a safe environment.

Learning experiences can either promote or inhibit the development of the foregoing values. Preservice teachers often want to stay with the comfortable, "clean," technical aspects of teaching without delving into the messier (and more realistic) ethical and personal dilemmas that teachers face daily. For example, they want to know "what works" in terms of classroom management. While such important concepts as proactive classroom management should be discussed, issues of fairness, equity, oppression, democratic values, the ethic of caring, and other value-laden aspects of classroom management must also be part of any teacher education curriculum.

Following are several strategies for integrating such values into learning activities for preservice teachers:

- Involve students in long-term science investigations that require patience, discussion, risk taking, honesty, and skepticism. This type of activity (see examples in Chapter Five) must recur repeatedly if students are to gain increased insight and to cumulate knowledge, skill, and appreciation.
- Create a classroom climate that is caring, flexible, personal, and respectful of student ideas and discourse.
- Include time in classes and clinical seminars for discussion of phenomena observed, dilemmas uncovered, teachable moments recognized, and other intriguing or puzzling events.
- Conduct case discussions based on written cases (Silverman and Welty, 1992), video episodes, or personal experiences; guide students in considering the personal and social justice aspects of such cases, not just their technical aspects.
- Use articles that discuss issues that challenge common student assumptions about learning—for example, the futility of trying to teach everything of importance, the overt and subtle inequities that encourage some children more than others to study

science, or national studies that reflect on factors influencing student motivation and achievement in science.

- Set teaching and advising policies that maintain the dignity of the individual student preparing to become a teacher.
- Encourage self-assessment of one's values through autobiographies, journals, discussion, and so forth.

We wish, with this last set of examples, to illustrate that the teaching of science, as all teaching, is a moral art that must reflect both the values of science and the values of a democratic society.

7

Designing an Effective
Preservice Program for Science

The following story illustrates the parallels between effective science education and effective teacher preparation. It suggests common beliefs and approaches that may form a foundation for future collaboration. Such collaborations can help focus attention on prospective teacher education programs as a whole, rather than on separate segments of teacher education programs. Improving the preparation of elementary school teachers in science requires that the many players in teacher education work together to reform entire programs.

Last night Ed, a geology professor, met Sally, an elementary teacher educator, at a cocktail party at the dean's house. Over the stuffed mushrooms, Ed mentioned to Sally that he had been in the field all day with the students from his Introduction to Geology course and was amazed to learn how many of them were headed to elementary classrooms.

"They're a very hostile audience," Ed said. "They come to me resenting even having to take science and thinking of it as totally irrelevant to their lives and their future teaching. I have to work really hard to help them see science as not only

relevant but as a powerful tool to help them teach everything better."

Sally's interest was aroused. "How have you approached that?" she asked. "I've always known that prospective elementary teachers typically hate science, and I've never been able to figure out what to do about it."

"Well, here's what I've been doing," Ed explained. "I've given up on the traditional course structure of teaching topics in geology, such as mineralogy, petrography, geomorphology, and so on. Instead, I begin my class each semester by soliciting from the students what they're really concerned about in their world that they think is related to science and technology. Based on this semester's information, we're investigating water pollution in the area. Then I give them some opportunities to discuss what they know about the problems, so I can understand where they're coming from and the foundation on which to build future learning."

"How interesting!" exclaimed Sally. "You probably do your professional reading in geology journals, but if you'd been reading ours, you'd have seen a lot recently about how critical it is to understand what learners bring to a new learning situation so you can help them develop or even reconstruct some of their understandings. You've been doing some of that—getting at what's called prior knowledge."

Ed smiled. "It stands to reason that you have to start where students are. What this means is that the way I used to teach science classes—and nearly all my science colleagues still do—is all wrong. I need to start with students' questions or concerns

*and then help them learn to be scientists in explor-
ing the areas of interest. That means they're out of
the classroom a lot—in the field, in the library, in
offices of government agencies, in labs of other
scientists. Instead of lecturing, I'm usually facilitating their work. They often work in groups too, as do
scientists."*

*"That's certainly where we in education are
heading," noted Sally. "We're very often in schools,
from the start of the professional sequence, helping
students get answers to some of their concerns, such
as what are schools like and whether the kids like
them. We're showing them ways to observe in classrooms, watching children and teachers do what
they do. That way their questions become more focused and can lead to an exploration of how children learn and teachers teach."*

*Ed pondered this for a moment. "That relates
directly to another thing I care about. I want students to carry away from my course an appreciation
for how we come to know things in science. For example, I want them to know how to ask good questions and how to gather evidence to answer them."*

*"Well, that's exactly what we hope for all
our students," replied Sally. "We discuss at great
length the idea of teachers being inquirers and decision makers. I wonder what else we have in common and how we might continue this conversation
with others who are interested. Given that we've
just begun to work on our accreditation, this might
be a way to break the mold in our design work for
the new teacher education program. How about
lunch next week sometime with Mike, another
science educator in our department, to see if there's
something to pursue?"*

Those who care about good science education in elementary schools—and preparing teachers to make it happen—are discovering real parallels in their approaches and real potential for working together. Just as good elementary schools are committed to "the whole child," good teacher education programs serve "the whole preservice teacher." Reform programs, rather than offering a collection of unconnected courses, try instead to provide a set of coordinated experiences that have a coherent vision, approach, and message. The whole must equal more than the sum of its parts. In the preceding vignette, the seed for such a program is being planted with the discovery of common beliefs and approaches that may form a firm foundation for a coherent program for the elementary education students at Ed and Sally's university.

Chapters Five and Six address the content and nature of the learning experiences likely to produce effective courses in science content and in science pedagogy for prospective elementary school teachers. In this chapter, we consider the program as a whole, in particular how the various parts can be effectively integrated. As is the case for our analysis and recommendations for the individual program components, here too we stress that there is no one "right" answer. Instead, a variety of alternative structures can accommodate the kinds of experiences discussed in the preceding chapters. We *can* say, however, that certain characteristic features of the science and science education components of teacher education programs as a whole are likely to distinguish effective programs from ineffective ones. We discuss these in the next section.

Characteristics of Effective Preservice Teacher Education Programs

We believe that the five characteristics listed below must be present in all teacher education programs in science regardless of their structure. After discussing these, we present and illustrate three different structural program configurations that incorporate all five characteristics, as well as the additional factors discussed in the preceding chapters on science content and pedagogy.

1. Both science content and science pedagogy are taught from an inquiry-based perspective.
2. Pedagogy is studied in the context of science content.
3. Collaboration between science faculty, education faculty, and experienced elementary teachers is integral to program design, integration, and implementation.
4. Elementary schools play a critical role in the teacher education process and the teaching of pedagogic content knowledge.
5. The transition from preservice to practice is smooth and consistent.

Inquiry-Based Perspective

The inquiry-based perspective is so important that it bears reemphasis with respect to a program's overall design. Just as science is a process of discovery, so too is science teaching. The objectives of a teacher preparation program in science should not just be to familiarize prospective teachers with available materials and resources. Prospective teachers need to learn how to ascertain what students already know by asking them appropriate questions; how to discover which strategies work and which do not under particular conditions—and why; how to recognize a teachable moment and how to use it to best advantage; how to use previous experiences as a guide for future practice; and how to communicate this knowledge to others. Prospective teachers should learn to consider each lesson as an opportunity to investigate the efficacy of an approach, the utility of an instructional material, the behavior of a student in response to a particular kind of directive.

Moreover, as future investigators, prospective teachers need to learn how to keep up-to-date with educational research, how to incorporate new findings into practice, and how to use these new findings as templates for further clinical investigation, perhaps in collaboration with university research colleagues. Such a view of teaching as inquiry should be modeled by teacher educators in their own teaching and should pervade the teacher education curriculum (Lampert and Ball, 1990; Osborne, 1993). Parallels between the investigative process in teaching and the investigative process of science should be made explicit, and the ideals of these processes of discovery should ultimately form the core pedagogical perspective and the essential educational objectives that prospective teachers eventually take with them into the elementary school classroom.

Four preservice teachers are sitting outside eating their lunch in the noon sunshine. Shanna has brought along a small oaktag sundial, which she made herself from a pattern provided as part of a local science museum activity packet. She always likes to try out activities before sharing them with the children, and so she sets the sundial down in the sunlight.

"Should the pointer be facing north or south?" Shanna asks the others. "Doesn't it have to point north to get a shadow if the sun's always in the south?" answers José.

Lisa jumps in: "Why wouldn't you get a shadow either way? It must have something to do with the position of the sun at noon. Isn't that why you can't just use a stick pushed straight into the ground? Now that I think of it, I never did understand why sundials always have the pointer tipped at an angle. How many degrees is this tilted? Is it right for where we are?"

"Our latitude is forty-three degrees. It seems about right. But that means this sundial pattern wouldn't be any good for people in Atlanta or Puerto Rico," José observes.

"Does the right tilt mean the shadow moves differently during the day than a straight up and down stick? Why would it? I think I'd have to watch it happen, you know, the two kinds sitting side by side, to be sure what happens," says Lisa.

Two others chime in, "Let's try it!"

The more the four talk, the more they realize

*how many questions they have. Although all of them
have a good science background, they chuckle,
realizing that their course work has not helped them
understand the sundial. But they are eager to figure
it out.*

*Later the same day, in their science methods
class, they ask Dr. Saskens to help them examine
how the sundial works and why. She replies that she
has some material they can read and suggests that
they collect a few different sundials and experiment
with them. "Maybe once you've had a chance to explore the sundial yourselves, this would be a good
topic to use for our next investigation with the
children."*

*The prospective teachers nod, thinking about
how much they have been learning during their
weekly exploration sessions with their own students.
The children's ideas are often very different from
what these prospective teachers expected. They are
amazed at how their own scientific understanding
has deepened as they have tried to make sense of
what the children are saying.*

Pedagogy in the Context of Content

Pedagogical devices such as the teaching/learning model, cooperative learning, and authentic assessments have proved to be powerful tools for facilitating science learning. However, while these
devices may be aptly described in the abstract, learning to apply
them requires study, discussion, and practice in the context of particular content examples. Just as scientific concepts are best taught
by having students reason from the concrete to the abstract, so too
the teaching of pedagogical concepts needs to be anchored in their
application to the teaching of science content. This is also true for
many aspects of classroom management, especially for the teaching
of inquiry-based science, where management strategies for conduct-

ing in-class investigations are essentially meaningless in the abstract.

For too long, methods courses—the traditional staple of professional education for teachers—have been criticized for their overemphasis on generic skills, the utility of which only becomes clear once specific situations have been encountered in actual classrooms. Instruction in pedagogy must work to develop judgment capabilities with respect to which strategies are likely to be appropriate for teaching particular subject matter in particular situations. In sum, instruction in pedagogy needs to be grounded in specific content. Enough field experiences must be provided, however, so that prospective teachers feel comfortable with the immediate issues of classroom management. When students feel sure of themselves in the classroom, they will begin to make the connections between content and pedagogy (Krajcik and others, 1993).

Collaboration Between Science Faculty, Education Faculty, and Experienced Elementary Teachers

Teaching is an interdisciplinary field. Good teaching involves the application of a knowledge base that melds with other knowledge bases—those of subject matter, psychology, and educational research, to name a few—each of which is in itself a domain worthy of full-time professional inquiry. Teaching borrows from all of them and channels relevant knowledge to the analysis and treatment of particular classroom situations. Just as architects develop facility in their profession not only through apprenticeships with masters but also by learning from engineers, draftspersons, mathematicians, artists, and historians, teachers develop facility in teaching not only through clinical apprenticeships but also through the convergence of numerous experiences from a variety of disciplinary perspectives.

Viewed in this way, teacher education must be a collaborative process. In the realm of science teaching in particular, scientists, education and science education faculty, and experienced teacher practitioners all contribute critical elements to this process. In assimilating and integrating these multiple perspectives, teacher education students reach an understanding that is larger than the sum of its parts. They become socialized into a new way of thinking—thinking like a professional *teacher*, able to access information from its sources, yet focused on translating that information into a form that students can at first investigate at their level and eventually assimilate for themselves.

For these collaborations truly to work, the relationships cannot be pro forma but must be based on a real commitment of all participants to prepare high-quality elementary school teachers. Participants must also have time to explore their common goals and communicate ideas over an extended period, during both the planning and teaching phases of science content and methods courses (Krajcik and others, 1993).

Schools in the Teacher Education Process

Teaching is a clinical practice. As such, a key aspect of learning to teach involves the acquisition of extensive experience in the classroom. Prospective teachers need to be able to reflect constantly on their study of science content, pedagogy, psychology, and the social context of education in light of their experiences in actual classroom situations. If prospective teachers are to gain multiple perspectives, there needs to be continuous interplay between theory and practice, involving ongoing discussions with both master teachers and university faculty members (Roth and others, 1992).

Higher education institutions and elementary schools must both play significant roles in the teacher education process and collaborate extensively throughout that process. Their contributions should be complementary and of equal importance.

Master elementary school teachers, selected for both their skill in working with children and their skill in working with teacher candidates, should be considered to be clinical faculty members, on par with faculty at teacher education institutions, with leadership roles in designing and implementing teacher education programs. Indeed, as David C. Berliner (1986) implies, only through the collaboration of university faculty and master teachers can significant progress in teacher education be made. Berliner argues that expert teachers have developed the methods of analysis and action that lead to effective teaching but that these processes are so automatic for them that they need the assistance of researchers to help express the processes to preservice teachers. According to J. Myron Atkin (1991), the pragmatic, action-oriented knowledge of teachers is more useful to preservice teachers than the generalized, theory-driven knowledge of professors. School administrators should consider active participation in teacher education to be a critical mission of the school system and should encourage and reward the best teachers in the system for actively participating in the teacher education process.

Transition from Preservice to Practice

As with any professional practice, teaching should be viewed as a lifelong process of reflection, education, and improvement. This process requires a commitment to keeping abreast of and contributing to the development of a professional knowledge base that is constantly evolving and expanding. Opportunities for the enhancement of practice, such as seminars, institutes, curriculum development groups, or study groups, should build on a solid foundation set by a practitioner's more formal professional education, with preservice and continuing education forming a seamless web of consistent educational experiences. Preservice education and continuing education for the experienced professional need to be consistent in their philosophies, reflecting consensus on the fundamental features of the dynamic knowledge base for teaching. New teachers should be able to apply the principles and habits of mind that they developed during the course of their preservice experiences by virtue of the support and encouragement they receive from their more experienced teacher colleagues. Prospective teachers need to feel that, by completing a preservice program, they are joining a community of teaching professionals—a community that models, values, supports, and in fact demands that new teachers apply the very principles and habits of mind emphasized in their preservice programs. Participation in such professional organizations as the National Science Teachers' Association (NSTA) and the Council for Elementary Science International (CESI) helps entering teachers become part of an active professional community; attending conferences and reading journals contribute to teachers' lifelong development.

Induction programs should take into account the different aspects of the institutions that make up the education community. Universities, for instance, might best be used to provide workshops for new teachers, training mentor teachers, and establishing support networks (Johnston and Kay, 1987). Schools, on the other hand, can help induct teacher candidates into the profession and assure them that what they learned about teaching in their preservice years constitutes the necessary first step in pursuing a lifelong commitment to the growth and development of effective learning communities. A survey of first-year teachers (Huling-Austin and Murphy, 1987) found that teachers who were part of an induction program were more confident about their effectiveness and happier about their careers than first-year teachers who had not been part of an induction program. For schools to be effective in this important process, they must have in place a support structure that provides guidance and encouragement to new teachers.

Table 7.1. Three Model Teacher Education Programs.

Brompton College	South Poseidon University	Capital State University
Four years	Three + two years	Fifth year
Redesigned under-graduate science for nonmajors	Content and methods taught together and coordinated by means of local science resources	Rigorous admission requirements, including laboratory sciences
Methods courses coordinated with fieldwork and early teaching experiences	Content and methods courses include fieldwork in schools	Year-long apprenticeship tied to methods seminars
Use of mentor teachers during student teaching	University faculty support during first year of teaching	Independent teaching research project monitored by joint committee of teachers and university faculty

Profiles of Alternative Program Structures

In this section, we present profiles of three very different teacher education program structures, each of which incorporates several of the features discussed earlier in this chapter as well as those discussed in Chapters Five and Six. The college or university that illustrates each structure (see Table 7.1) is a composite built from actual programs examined in our study of teacher education programs (see Appendix and also Michelsohn and Hawkins, 1993). As such, these programs represent important steps forward but still fall short in some respects, particularly in the extent to which students are involved in the actual doing of science.

Brompton College

> *Overview:* Brompton College offers a "standard" four-year undergraduate program that encourages students to take additional liberal arts courses and extend their program to five years. Revised undergraduate science courses focus on a small number of real-world questions. Experience with children begins early.

Brompton College is located in a college town situated approximately one hundred miles from a major inland urban center. Its school of education offers a wide variety of educational degree programs and grants approximately two hundred bachelor's degrees in elementary education each year. The college recently adopted a new policy stressing the importance of a liberal arts education for elementary school teaching and, in so doing, has begun recommending that students preparing to be elementary school teachers concentrate and perhaps major in a liberal arts area, extending their stay at the college by one year.

The college has instituted other reforms in its teacher education program as well. For example, the traditional course on the social and historical foundations of education, originally given during the early phase of professional course work, was reconfigured as a capstone seminar to be taken near the end of the program. Notably, the college launched a sustained effort to collaborate with faculty in the college of arts and sciences and conferred clinical faculty status on a select group of master school teachers with whom the college had worked closely in the past. The college made a

strong commitment to playing a leadership role in teacher education reform, responding to requests from funding agencies for grant
proposals that stress the forging of close alliances among diverse
faculty and between universities and schools. To facilitate the in-
stitutionalization of these alliances, the university set up a campus-
wide teaching and learning center. At this center, faculty from
across the university can meet informally, attend seminars related
to teaching, and access print- and technology-based instructional
materials and resources.

To design and implement changes in its elementary school
teacher preparation program, the college formed an oversight committee made up of university and school faculty and administrators.
This committee in turn appointed a subcommittee of two scientists,
two science education faculty members, one education faculty
member interested in educational leadership, and two elementary
school teachers to work specifically on the reform of the science
component of the teacher education program. The faculty member
interested in educational leadership served as a liaison to the oversight committee, which was responsible for the reform of the overall
teacher education program. This arrangement helped ensure that
reforms in the science component would be consistent with the
reforms in progress for the program as a whole.

The college settled on a program design that in many ways
is traditional in its configuration: general liberal arts education
followed by professional courses followed by student teaching.
However, the program stresses the need for exposing teacher education students to children and to issues of cognitive development
early in the program by means of a comprehensive introductory
course in child development, with extensive field experiences, during the sophomore year. Field-based experiences were also introduced into all of the methods courses in the form of a practicum.
Students in the program now take four content-specific methods
courses: Teaching Children to Read and Write, Teaching Children
Mathematics, Teaching Children Science, and Teaching Children
Social Studies. These courses, which can be taken in any order, are
preceded by a new course, called Classroom Dynamics. This course
covers basic principles of planning and classroom management,
using video materials of actual classroom situations as a basis for

discussion, and also provides experiences in actual classrooms. Many of the topics previously covered in a general methods course are now taken up in context in the content-specific methods courses.

The science component of the teacher preparation program has three phases. In the first phase, students in the program are required to take three (and encouraged to take four) semesters of science. Science courses are offered through the college of arts and sciences and were designed in an overall university effort to reform undergraduate science teaching. The arts and sciences faculty consulted with professors in the school of education about effective teaching strategies and contemporary educational philosophies and approaches. They then tailored courses for nonscience majors that are nevertheless rigorous with respect to their development of scientific thinking and habits of mind, using teacher education students as a model audience. The collaboration also gave the education faculty a good understanding of the science background that their students would bring to the science methods course.

Four new one-semester science courses were designed, one each in biology, chemistry, physics, and earth and environmental sciences. Each course focuses on three basic themes that tie the science to major issues in society and everyday life and that address such broad concepts as systems, change, and diversity. The physics course, for example, addresses navigation, the age of the universe, and broadcasting as its major themes; the biology course considers the topics of birth defects, the physiology of dinosaurs, and the cellular basis of behavior. Each theme or topic in turn focuses on a hands-on research project designed to develop basic scientific concepts as well as more general related issues. In the portion of the physics course on the age of the universe, for example, students build their own telescopes, choose a celestial body to investigate, and then work on ways to determine the distance of that celestial body from the earth. Measuring such distances relates directly to questions about the size and consequently the age of the universe. Using their own observations and data from other astronomical studies, the students discuss the diversity of celestial bodies throughout the universe, how celestial bodies are organized into systems, and how the universe has changed and is likely to change in the future. Throughout each of the four courses, students work in small groups and are encouraged to dialogue extensively and focus on themselves as learners.

The second phase of the science component of the teacher education program consists of the science methods course and an associated practicum. In this course, students focus on the teaching of a small number of topics that are common to the elementary school science curriculum: life cycles, motion, basic chemical analysis, and weather. Students approach each topic as investigators, learning from their experiences many of the concepts that are often taught through lecture and readings in other methods courses. They investigate their own conceptions of the subject matter and how they came to acquire them; they interview elementary school students to determine the children's conceptions (and in doing so hone their questioning skills); they observe the teaching of the topic on video or, where possible, in actual classrooms and investigate the dynamics of the classroom situations; they analyze various instructional materials with respect to the presentation of the topic; and they design their own instructional unit and assessment. The students teach the unit to a group of six elementary school children on designated "small group teach-in days" at local elementary schools that participate in the implementation of the university-based teacher education program. Finally, the students evaluate their performance and the performance of their peers. Parallels between inquiry-based science and inquiry-based teaching are made explicit. The investigative approach to teaching methods has also been adopted in each of the other three content-specific methods courses, thus reinforcing the notion of teacher as inquirer throughout the program.

The third phase of the science component of the teacher education program is fully integrated with the program as a whole. During the final semester, teacher education students work almost full-time in local area schools, gradually taking on increasing teaching responsibilities under the guidance of mentor teachers who have been involved in the methods courses throughout the program.

Mentor teachers work with student teachers not only to acclimate them to the realities of day-to-day teaching but also to introduce them to the particulars of subject-specific pedagogy. Thus, at certain times during the course of the semester, mentor teachers will work with student teachers specifically on improving their science teaching, while at other times, they will work specifically on issues concerning the teaching of reading. Overall, however, emphasis is placed on integrating subjects where appropriate—for example, on finding ways to write across the curriculum or to use history as a context for discussing science and vice versa. Master teachers model this behavior in their own teaching and cultivate it in their apprentices. Along with their experiences in the classroom, the student teachers attend a seminar on the social and historical foundations of education and meet weekly with their mentor teachers to reflect on their practice and assess their progress.

South Poseidon University

> *Overview:* South Poseidon University offers a "3+2" program with a concentrated science component. The science component of the program consists of an intensive, one-semester focus on both science content and science pedagogy with one overarching theme.

Southern Poseidon University (SPU), located near an urban seaport, was originally a normal school but has since grown into a large research and teaching institution with a student population approaching twenty thousand. SPU has a strong faculty in marine science and oceanography and a partnership with local industry to train technicians to use increasingly sophisticated automated equipment. The university's locale is home as well to a science museum and an aquarium, both of which also conduct original research.

The university has approximately thirty-five faculty members in its school of education and graduates approximately two hundred elementary education majors each year. The school of education recently embarked on a multifaceted effort to reform its teacher education program. In particular, it incorporated changes in the science component of the curriculum that build upon the particular strengths and resources available at the university.

The program was developed by a committee made up of

members of the arts and sciences faculty, the faculty of education, local elementary school teachers and administrators, and representatives from the science museum and the aquarium. SPU's program for prospective elementary school teachers previously took place during the junior and senior undergraduate years. However, the administration instituted instead a "3+2" program whereby students spend their first three years concentrating on a liberal arts education and the following two years pursuing a professional course of study. In addition, while the overall structure of a general liberal arts education followed by professional education remains effectively in place, the organization of course work during the last two years was altered radically. The science component of the program serves as a focus for program integration during the second semester of the fourth year, when elementary education majors spend the majority of their time engaged in projects and activities related to science, science teaching, and integrating the teaching of science with the teaching of other subject areas.

Using the museum and aquarium facilities, students investigate a small number of interdisciplinary topics in depth from multiple perspectives. For example, students choose from among a number of marine ecologies in which to study the diversity of organisms and then discuss the diversity of ways that different cultures use and interact with marine life in their societies and economies. In another unit, students investigate the physics of sonar in the context of studying dolphin navigation. They then discuss issues of navigation in a broader context, solving problems in geometry, using astronomical observations to track ships at sea, and relating the discussion to how early explorers investigated world geography. In still another unit, students study how nerve impulses control digestive behaviors in the lobster and then discuss the ionic basis of the nerve impulses in the broader context of the chemistry underlying how batteries work.

Each of the units relates in some way to an exhibit currently on display or in the design stages at the science museum, and laboratory facilities are made available to students at the aquarium. In addition, the museum and aquarium both participate in an inservice teacher education program in which teachers from the local school district spend one month each summer working with museum and aquarium staff members to adapt exhibits for classroom use. A catalogue of adaptations is then made available to preservice teachers, who, as part of their semester-long science program, discuss ways to translate their experiences into experiences appropriate for elementary school children. Some of the teachers who have participated in the in-service program in the past are invited to participate in seminars and discussions with preservice teachers to help foster a continuum between preservice and continuing teacher education.

In addition to the seminars and discussions with classroom teachers, each of the science units in the program includes a methods seminar and practicum. During the seminar and practicum, prospective teachers investigate in detail what instructional strategies and resources are available to build a bridge between their science experiences and actual elementary school classrooms. Teacher education students also use new interactive multimedia software to familiarize themselves with a variety of classroom science teaching situations and hold discussions about these situations. A variety of activities also offer teacher education students opportunities to create and synthesize their own resources. In addition, students spend the following summer working as docents in the museum, practicing their teaching skills while presenting exhibits to children who come to the museum for summer tours.

The science component of the professional teacher education program at SPU is set in the context of a more traditional teacher education program, in which elementary education majors complete their general education requirements and then take methods courses in reading and mathematics, along with a course in the social foundations of education, and complete the program with student teaching. However, plans are currently underway at SPU to make teacher education more modular and integrative, akin to the newly developed science component. The first semester of the fifth year, for example, is slated to focus on issues of world history, geography, and sociology but with components relating these subject areas to other disciplines, such as mathematics and science. The final semester is currently planned as an internship in which students gradually take on increasing teaching responsibilities while attending a weekly seminar on writing across the curriculum and a biweekly discussion group on reflective practice.

Following the formal teacher education program, many SPU teacher education graduates remain in the general geographic area. Each graduate's progress during the subsequent first year of teaching is supported by faculty at the SPU school of education. In addition, graduates are encouraged to continue to use the museum and aquarium facilities in their own teaching and to contribute as assistants and tutors to both the preservice and in-service science programs. Those graduates who leave the region are encouraged to contact local science museums and other science-related resources and work to incorporate them into their teaching.

Capital State University

> *Overview:* Capital State University offers a fifth-year internship/apprenticeship program, and entering students must have a B.A. degree. Much time is spent in local schools. The program also includes an introductory seminar and course work prior to the apprenticeship and a research project, follow-up course work, and seminars following it.

Capital State University, located in a rural state capital, has a student body approaching forty thousand and a large school of education with an international reputation for its educational research. Four years ago, the school of education replaced its baccalaureate elementary school teacher education program with a fifth-year graduate program leading to the degree of Master of Teaching. The program was designed in close collaboration with a number of area schools that offered to place teacher education at the forefront of their educational agenda in an effort to create a research-oriented learning community able to sustain a long-term commitment to educational reform. Arrangements were also made for members of the arts and sciences faculty to contribute to the program as student advisers.

The school adopted a stringent and rigorous application process for admission to the teacher education program. To gain admittance, students are required to have completed a bachelor's degree with a major or concentration in a liberal arts area and a grade-point average of at least 3.0; to have participated in community service; and to have worked with children in an institutional setting. In addition, students are required to have taken at least nine semester hours of natural sciences courses with laboratories, at least one course each in the physical and life sciences, at least nine semester hours in history or geography, at least six semester hours in college-level mathematics, at least six semester hours of developmental and cognitive psychology, and at least six semester hours of college-level English and writing courses. Student applicants must also complete a performance-based entrance examination that assesses subject matter knowledge and be interviewed by the faculty.

The program begins during the first week of August with a month-long component to prepare students for the beginning of the school year. During this time, students take a seminar on classroom dynamics that employs interactive multimedia software to allow investigations of a variety of classroom situations, a seminar on school context and curriculum offered by administrators from schools participating in the teacher education program, and a reading seminar on child psychology and cognitive development as they apply to the teaching of basic quantitative and verbal concepts and in which students relate their discussions to the situations encountered in their classroom dynamics seminar.

Once the school year begins, teacher education students apprentice with individual master teachers, spending approximately half of their time working with the teacher in the classroom. Students initially observe the class and help the teacher set up the classroom, correct papers, and tutor individual children. Over time, teacher education students take on increasing classroom responsibilities. They also collect data on individual students' performances—using worksheets, projects, journals, and assessments—and follow these students' progress over the course of the year. Each day, the teacher education student meets with the classroom teacher to discuss the day's events and the consequences for future planning. Each master teacher is assigned three to four teacher education students for the year, and these students form a cohesive working cohort.

In addition to apprenticing with one teacher, each student in the teacher education program assembles an advisory committee consisting of four members: the master teacher, one other teacher, a faculty member from the school of education, and a faculty member from the college of arts and sciences. The committee monitors the student's progress through the program and works with the student to develop an independent research project that focuses on the teaching of a particular subject area. (Students may choose members of the committee who have a particular interest in that subject.) This project is carried out during the course of the school year and is written up for presentation to fellow students and for defense before the advisory committee.

In addition to spending half of their time apprenticing in individual classrooms and additional time each week working on their independent research project, students engage in course work and the observation of other classes. Students take a series of seminars—conducted by education faculty from the university in collaboration with teachers at the school—on subject-specific pedagogy, in which they focus on the teaching of a particular subject relevant to their apprenticeship. During the science pedagogy seminar, for example, students investigate the conceptions that their own students have about the science topics they are studying, observe other classes engaged in science learning and explore how changes in students' cognitive abilities affect the nature of the science curriculum at different levels of development, discuss how to integrate science topics with other aspects of the curriculum, and relate their seminar work to real-life classroom teaching by working with their mentor teacher to plan and help teach actual science lessons. The teaching behaviors discussed in the pedagogy seminars are modeled by the master teachers in the program, and the teacher education students are able to observe these behaviors on a day-to-day basis.

By the end of the school year, teacher education students begin to take on full-time classroom responsibilities, with the mentor teacher serving as critic and coach. Thus, the elementary school students are nurtured by a dedicated group of four or five adults who are committed to supporting their learning potential and their growth as individuals.

During the summer following the school year, teacher education students complete their individual research projects. They assemble and analyze the data they have accumulated over the course of the year and pool their data with the data accumulated by the other two or three members of their cohort who share the same master teacher. Together, the cohort members make a presentation to their peers and instructors on the progress of the elementary class over the course of the year. The program culminates with the presentation by each teacher education student of a report on his or her individual research project and a defense of the work before his or her advisory committee. The committee gives a final evaluation of the student's overall work at the end of the program.

Key Design Considerations

As the foregoing composites of actual practices and Tyson's (1994) examples show, good preservice education can occur within a variety of structures. Even the traditional structure of relatively unconnected courses—in which students start with content courses, then take education courses, and finish with student teaching—can incorporate inquiry-based science, content-oriented methods courses, and field experiences under conditions that encourage reflection through exchanges with mentor teachers and other guides. This kind of program probably works best when the choice of courses is somewhat constrained.

Effective programs occur more often when content and pedagogy courses are taught together or are highly coordinated. Usually, this requires students to take the courses in a fixed order. In programs that stress internships or apprenticeships, teacher education students spend most of their pedagogy course time working and studying in elementary schools with classroom teachers; often, their university courses are taught in the elementary school building as well.

Two other factors are more critical than the precise program structure for the effective preservice science education of prospective elementary school teachers. First and foremost, the design of the program should incorporate generative models of instruction that follow a constructivist approach. That is, students should first be encouraged to explore a topic (whether in science or in the science learning of children), to get some hands-on experience (through science inquiry or microteaching), and to receive help in making meaning out of that experience in their science or methods class; then they should be required to take action based on their deepened understanding, action that may involve pursuing their science inquiry in greater depth or revising relevant aspects of their teaching.

The second critical factor is collaboration between university faculty members and between institutions of higher education and local schools. At a minimum, there should be informal collaboration between individuals or general institutional collaboration on such issues as distribution requirements. More effective, though more difficult to institute, is joint planning, as, for example, when science and education faculty members and elementary school teachers collaboratively develop science content or pedagogy courses. Even closer integration occurs when the collaborators involved jointly implement their plans across the whole program, including science content courses, methods courses, and field experiences. Often, such implementation includes collaborative research as well. An interesting setting for collaborative program planning, implementation, and research is the professional development school, a school in which elementary school teachers are in active partnership with university faculty in working with student teachers and in improving both the elementary school and the teacher education program.

8

Recommendations

In this chapter, we make recommendations on reforming the science preparation of prospective elementary school teachers, while noting some of the barriers and inhibiting factors to reform. Our first set of recommendations deals with the need for a systemic approach. The recommendations are grouped according to the communities that have specific responsibilities for the science education of prospective elementary school teachers. We believe, however, that these groups must take action simultaneously and collaboratively if any one recommendation is to be put into effect. We therefore urge that our recommendations for teacher education reform not be considered in isolation but as a whole. ⁾

Our second set of recommendations is more general, designed to build consensus on the importance of (1) science education in elementary school and (2) the preservice education of elementary school teachers. In our view, improvement will only be possible when there is much more widespread agreement on and support for these two issues. We urge a concerted effort to highlight the need for placing a high priority on both.

A Systemic Approach

Responsibility for the reform of science instruction in the schools and science preservice education, which are inevitably linked, lies not with a single group of individuals but with several groups that need to function as collaborators in planning and implementing changes. One change in a system may alter a local condition but leave the system itself largely unperturbed; more often, other parts of the system will counteract even local change. A planned, coordinated intervention at several points is more likely to succeed. For example, one might suggest that school districts institute more flexible scheduling to allow more time for science, but if teachers dislike science and feel ill prepared to teach it, then increasing the time allocated for teaching science will change little in the classroom and even less in children's ultimate science learning. Ideally, as districts change local conditions to allow more time for science, colleges and universities will be developing teachers—through both preservice and in-service programs—who have a zest for teaching science and can do so effectively.

Another aspect of the need for a systemic approach is the obvious fact that effective preparation for teaching science in elementary school needs to be part of the general preparation of prospective elementary school teachers. Changes in the teaching of science in elementary schools will not occur without concurrent changes in the teaching of reading and language arts, mathematics, social studies, and other subjects. Likewise, changes in preservice science education cannot take place without concomitant changes in other areas of the preservice program. Hence, we have tried to set our recommendations for science education in the larger context of the overall preservice education program for prospective elementary school teachers.

We have framed our recommendations from two different perspectives: what a stakeholder group can do by itself and what two or more stakeholder groups can do collaboratively. Although in no way approaching a systemic implementation plan, these joint recommendations point out that change must occur in multiple arenas. In the recommendations that follow, we start with the groups most directly involved in teacher preservice education—the colleges and universities and their faculties—and proceed to those who are involved at a more peripheral level—the states and professional organizations.

Improving College/University Teaching

Three groups of professors, those responsible for general education courses, those responsible for science methods courses, and those responsible for science courses, are integral to advancing excellence in the science education of prospective elementary school teachers. While each of these groups faces specific problems, there are several common areas of their practice that need to change, no matter what their teaching assignment. First and foremost, they must model exemplary teaching. If the lecture-and-test method is used exclusively, it is unlikely that future teachers will internalize a range of good teaching strategies. If they hear about such strategies at all, they may learn them only at the memory level, devoid of any meaningful real-life teaching context. The need to model both the doing of science and the effective teaching of science is especially critical for science faculty. The teaching styles that these faculty exhibit may be more influential than those of the science methods faculty because the science content courses will set the standard in the students' minds for the teaching of science.

A related issue concerns the system for promoting and rewarding university faculty. Typically, university reward systems emphasize scholarship and research over good teaching. This is equally true for all three groups of faculty mentioned above. Fortunately, some recent trends support excellence in college teaching and challenge the traditional reward systems, at least for education faculty. Many universities are promoting faculty development, clearer learning outcomes, and more systematic assessment of learning. Ernest E. Boyer (1987) suggests that inquiry into the results of one's own teaching be considered a legitimate area of "scholarship." Such journals as the *Journal of College Teaching* and the *Journal of College Science Teaching* emphasize college teaching and classroom research (Cross, 1987), and education professors are being encouraged to focus their research on teacher preparation and the effects of their teaching. The latest NCATE guidelines also support the improvement of college teaching.

Furthermore, colleges of education are being required to increase the involvement of professors in preservice students' clinical experiences in schools. This will affect the general education faculty who teach the professional core courses, such as educational psychology, general teaching methods, social foundations, and measurement; but it will affect the faculty who teach content-specific methods courses even more. Indeed, the California legislature has enacted legislation that requires recent in-school experience for professors assigned to teaching methods courses.

Who are the professors teaching methods courses? In the case of science, they are either science department faculty or teacher education faculty. The science professor may or may not have experience in or knowledge of elementary teaching. The education professor may or may not have experience in or knowledge of a particular field of science. Of course, the worst example is the professor who lacks expertise in either science or education. The best example is the professor who is both a scientist *and* a teacher educator.

In some universities, content-area methods courses are taught in the academic department by professors who specialize in education. In other places, the education professors specialize in science methods. We see both situations as potentially effective as long as the professors model good teaching and help students understand science *and* learn methods of science teaching. Innovative communication mechanisms, such as those used by the Project to Improve Methods Courses in Elementary Science, spearheaded by California State University at Long Beach, can bring together science content faculty and science methods faculty to share reform ideas and rethink courses.

Faculty members responsible for teaching science methods courses can be involved with clinical experiences in the schools through student teaching supervision, microteaching opportunities, professional development schools, and action research projects. The more university faculty are involved with elementary science classrooms, the more likely it will be that the university experiences of prospective elementary school teachers will be of high quality.

Led by high-ranking administrators, postsecondary institutions should adopt the improvement of teaching practice in both science and education as a top priority and consider excellent teaching to be an integral part of the mission of the institution. Our first three recommendations address this area.

As a result of the education reforms of the 1980s, tremendous emphasis has been placed on improving the delivery of instruction in K–12 institutions. Postsecondary institutions, however, have not benefited from the same degree of scrutiny of their instructional processes. As the contributions of cognitive science have started to blur some of the traditional distinctions between pedagogy and adult education, similarities and differences are emerging between teaching children, young people, and adults. For this reason, we believe a center for model teaching and learning at all levels could be a great resource for postsecondary institutions. Since this would be too large an investment for many institutions, we also provide a second example, a colloquium, as a way to begin dialogue and heighten awareness of effective teaching strategies for different types of learners. Both these mechanisms are intended to encourage post-secondary faculty to become inquiring learners who seek to improve their own teaching.

> **Recommendation:** University leaders should facilitate a university-wide emphasis on the improvement of teaching practice in their institution by creating university-wide opportunities for faculty to discuss and improve their practice. This might be accomplished, for example, through the creation of college/ university-wide teaching and learning centers for faculty that focus on the use of mentors, student observers, class visits by peers, and other evaluation techniques or the creation of college/university-wide colloquia on science, science education, and human values.

More specifically, science faculty must be made aware of the disjunction between the current ways of university science teaching and what is known about effective practice. They must be encouraged to adopt an active, student-centered approach to science learning in all undergraduate and graduate science courses. It is especially important that students who are not likely to be exposed to advanced science courses, including such nonmajors as prospective elementary school teachers, have the opportunity to engage in authentic science inquiry.

> **Recommendation:** Science faculty should redesign undergraduate science courses so that they stress broad themes, habits of mind, and scientific thinking. "Introductory" science courses should be designed as self-contained courses rather than simply as prerequisites to more advanced courses; that is, students in such basic courses should be able to study compelling phenomena and tackle meaningful problems rather than focus on abstract, rudimentary principles out of context.

If teaching at the postsecondary level is to change, a different reward structure is going to have to be put in place in universities. Many postsecondary institutions, especially research universities, have had a long history of acknowledging the need for effective instruction but actually rewarding staff not for their teaching but for their publications and research accomplishments. Although good instruction is in no way an end in itself, it is a prerequisite for effective learning for most students. Moreover, it is important for ensuring an adequate supply of new students, graduate students, and ultimately researchers.

> **Recommendation:** University leaders should reward excellent university teaching practice with promotions, awards, tenure, and remuneration.

Institutions of Higher Education and Schools

Schools are in a period of flux. Many schools are involved in improvement efforts that give more leadership to the school staff and parents. Many more schools, however, are run in more traditional ways. The challenge is to prepare teachers who will be able to work in either one of these environments. If schools do indeed restructure around the site-based management concept, they will need teachers who are reflective, confident, and competent. It is difficult to imagine a restructured school without empowered teachers. Therefore, one job of teacher educators is to help new teachers understand the processes of organizational change and school governance. With such preparation, they are ready for the responsibility of collaborative school planning and management.

But what of the teachers who begin their careers in schools where little change or improvement is under way? The structures and operations of a good many schools impede new teachers from implementing some of the research-based practices they have learned at the university. Lack of manipulative materials for science lessons; uninspired curriculum guides and units; expectations of "content coverage"; grading, tracking, and grouping practices; and parents' preconceptions of "good teaching" can all thwart the creativity and enthusiasm of new teachers.

Teachers must be prepared to survive within less-than-perfect systems *and* to participate fully in innovative environments. In addition to practice in using up-to-date science programs, teachers probably need practice in how to adapt older materials and curricula for greater effectiveness. Because of this challenge, it is important to develop teachers who are able to design and adapt units of study rather than merely use what is handed to them.

Science, science education, and elementary education university faculty must work together with elementary school classroom teachers to develop a consensus vision of what elementary school teachers of science need to know and be able to do. After developing their vision, these groups must collaborate on the planning, organization, and implementation of the science and science education components of preservice teacher education programs. To help foster such collaborations, science faculty, education faculty, and classroom teachers should be encouraged to engage each other in conversations on topics of mutual interest and in other social and professional interactions. More formal mechanisms are needed for joint program planning and implementation. The next half-dozen recommendations pertain to such mechanisms.

Recommendation: The different faculties involved in teacher education should agree, together with experienced elementary school teachers, on a set of learning principles and activities that will enable prospective elementary school teachers to develop the competencies and behaviors necessary for effective science teaching. Any set of principles and activities should include the following two: (1) science content and science pedagogy experiences will be appropriately coordinated, as discussed in this book, and (2) prospective elementary school teachers will be helped to develop an appropriate understanding of scientific thought through a variety of experiences in which they engage in at least one in-depth scientific investigation, preferably combining the natural and social sciences, as illustrated in the erosion example in Chapter Five.

Recommendation: Top-level college or university and school district administrators should convene local area study panels with policy- and decision-making authority to mandate change in the practice of preservice science education for elementary school teachers. Study panels should consist of university faculty from both the arts and sciences and education, university and school district administrators, and elementary school teachers.

Recommendation: To implement their collective vision of appropriate science preparation for prospective elementary school teachers, the study panel should identify and appoint (or cause to be appointed) key people to implement its policies. Individuals charged with implementation must be skilled at exercising leadership in a collaborative environment.

Recommendation: Top-level college or university and school district administrators should encourage science faculty, education faculty, and classroom teachers to collaborate with each other in the design and implementation of preservice science programs by rewarding such collaboration with promotions, awards, tenure, and other substantive incentives.

It is difficult to prepare elementary school teachers to teach science (or any subject) well without having them practice with excellent clinical teachers in classrooms. Yet forging meaningful partnerships with schools can be challenging for colleges and universities. Teachers are already very busy, and only a few see preparing future teachers as an important part of their job. Often, student teachers are accepted because they will lend an extra "pair of hands" in the classroom. Or, worse, the principal assigns student teachers to teachers who are so weak that they need the assistance of a student teacher. Such experiences are not likely to produce excellent teachers.

Even when teachers are willing to take on the important supervising role, how are they prepared for it? Typically, there is little preparation other than reading a handbook that outlines procedures and a suggested schedule. In some places, teachers must participate in a staff development program before they may have a student teacher. This is a step in the right direction. For elementary teachers of science, however, more is needed. The science teacher educator, classroom teacher, and student teacher should work together to examine the science curriculum, analyze the pedagogical content knowledge required, review the characteristics of the learners, and clarify content and methods. A good place to begin may be with the popular topic of "teaching thinking" because many elementary teachers may not realize how powerful science lessons can be for developing higher-level thinking skills.

Unfortunately, the haphazard nature of student teaching programs frequently precludes such coordination. Most large programs have a separate office for student teaching, which is divorced from the rest of the teacher education program. Because of this structure, conceptual coherence between courses and clinical experiences is rare. It is not uncommon for the faculty who teach methods courses never to set foot in a clinical classroom—hence the California legislation. Often, lecturers or graduate students who have little knowledge of the content of the formal science or science methods courses are the ones supervising student teaching. This neglect of the final—and critically important—stage of teacher preparation is a major problem.

> **Recommendation:** Each school district, in consultation with local colleges or universities, should develop at least one professional development school, in which science is valued and science teaching is exemplary, to serve as a clinical setting for teacher education programs in science.

> **Recommendation:** University and school administrators must institute training to prepare both college and classroom teachers for their role as supervisors of student teachers or interns.

State Policies

Many states are implementing reforms in teacher preparation in the areas of science and mathematics. For example, the Massachusetts Department of Education has proposed changes in the preservice training of teachers to take effect in October 1994. A teacher can be certified as a teacher of general science for grades five through nine or nine through twelve. Provisional certification will require (1) a bachelor's degree with a major in the liberal arts and sciences or an interdisciplinary major; (2) completion of course work or other experiences that address subject matter knowledge in each of the sciences, modes of inquiry and methods of research, use of computers, and relationships among the sciences and between the sciences and mathematics and other fields of knowledge; (3) completion of a prepracticum; and (4) successful completion of a practicum judged on the basis of demonstrated ability to teach in the area of the general science certificate and the "common teaching standards" defined by the state. Full certification will require completion of a post-baccalaureate clinical experience and of a master's degree program that may include (but does not require) graduate course work in the sciences and pedagogical content knowledge.

Even in this two-stage model that requires a major in a content area other than education, the science requirement is entirely in the hands of the individual institution granting the bachelor's degree. One can safely assume that a student will take one or possibly two science courses for graduation, but it seems entirely possible that a student may begin teaching without broad exposure to the fields of science. Massachusetts will require "demonstrated ability" to teach in the area of science, but what kind of ability must be demonstrated is not well defined. It seems unlikely that teachers will enter elementary classrooms in the state any more confident of their grasp of science content knowledge than is the case under the system that is being replaced. To improve science instruction at the elementary level, distribution requirements in science content areas to be met during the undergraduate or graduate program should be instituted, standards for content and pedagogical content knowledge should be articulated in detail, and prospective teachers' science content and science teaching knowledge should be assessed. Our next two recommendations address certification and induction issues.

> **Recommendation:** State boards of education should mandate that all prospective elementary school teachers must have appropriate training in both science content and science pedagogy. Standards must be specified in sufficient detail to ensure high-quality teacher preparation programs. Specifications might include the successful completion of sixteen semester hours of laboratory/field science or the equivalent and the successful completion of science pedagogy courses that include investigative and reflective experiences as discussed in this book, including exposure to diverse groups of students. Such "successful completion" should be determined by performance-based assessments in both science and science teaching, matching the behaviors described in this book.

> **Recommendation:** State boards of education, in collaboration with the National Council for Accreditation of Teacher Education, should require a core emphasis on science content and science methods for accreditation

of all elementary school teacher education programs. Such accreditation should require programs to provide adequate and appropriate opportunities for prospective elementary school teachers to develop knowledge and skill in the teaching of science, as outlined in this book.

Professional Societies and Organizations

Although most professional societies are not directly involved in teacher preparation, they should exercise their collective voice and influence in bringing about improvement.

> **Recommendation:** Scientific and educational professional organizations should collaborate to produce and publish a document that includes at least ten definitive statements that define a new vision for preservice elementary school teacher education in science; these statements should be robustly contrasted with descriptions of current programs. The document should also contain a set of guidelines for a consensus-building process that can be used at state and local levels.

> **Recommendation:** The leadership of major scientific and educational professional organizations should issue joint statements, made available to the press and the public, on the need for preservice teacher education reform in science. They should follow up by encouraging the collaboration of their constituencies in designing and carrying out innovative projects to reform preservice programs.

Our third recommendation in this area, we believe, would serve not only the cause of better science education for prospective teachers but also the cause of better science education for all college undergraduates, whether or not they subsequently choose to become science majors.

> **Recommendation:** Major scientific organizations should emulate the National Research Council and convene national panels of science professors and science educators to restructure undergraduate science courses.

Need for Consensus on Key Issues

The need for reform of programs preparing prospective elementary school teachers in science will not be given high priority until science instruction itself is given high priority in elementary classrooms. Science must take its place beside reading, language arts, and mathematics in the amount of time and resources allocated. All students need science, not just the academically and socially elite, and they need a sound beginning in elementary school.

To move parents, teachers, teacher educators, policy makers, and students themselves toward this point of view, we recommend the following actions.

> **Recommendation:** School districts and schools must reorganize to institute flexible schedules and improved working conditions for teachers to allow authentic science teaching and reflection on teaching practice, as discussed in this book.

> **Recommendation:** Major educational organizations, agencies, and policy-making bodies, such as the U.S. Department of Education, the National Education Association and American Federation of Teachers, the National Science Foundation, the National Science Teachers Association, the Association of Elementary School Principals, and the Council of Chief State School Officers, should issue joint policy statements advocating science as an essential core subject in the elementary school curriculum.

> **Recommendation:** The foregoing agencies and organizations, joined by the National Board for Professional Teaching Standards, the Association for

Educators of Teachers of Science, and the National Council for Accreditation of Teacher Education, should issue additional statements and hold public policy forums attesting to the fact that rigorous, high-quality preservice elementary school teacher education in science is an essential ingredient for the development of a new generation of scientifically literate Americans.

A pervasive American myth is that teachers are born, not made. In spite of evidence that people can be taught to be effective teachers, there is still a widespread belief that the core ability to teach is somehow innate.

Teaching is a professional practice that requires an education for professionals. This is as true of teachers as it is of doctors or engineers. Just as most people would have reservations about receiving a diagnosis and prescription for a serious physical problem from someone who had no medical training, they should feel equally uncomfortable with teachers who have not received an education anchored in content knowledge, content pedagogy, multiculturalism, an understanding of children's development, classroom dynamics, and social responsibility.

Recommendation: The president of the United States and the secretary of education should use their positions to highlight for the general public how teacher education reform and the professionalization of teaching are critical to the reform of science education. Public service announcements and aggressive marketing techniques could further educate the public as to the importance of science education.

Recommendation: The National Science Foundation and the U.S. Department of Education should set as a priority the funding of programs to improve the preservice science education of elementary school teachers. Such programs might include (1) the development of videotapes that illustrate the three areas in which the greatest change is needed: science content courses, science methods courses, and the final teacher preparation experience (student teaching); (2) the institution of a national award program for outstanding teacher education in science (both for institutions and individuals), using criteria for excellence such as those proposed in this book; and (3) innovations in faculty development that foster exemplary teaching in science content and methods courses and the collaboration of scientists, science educators, elementary educators, and elementary school teachers.

Recommendation: Philanthropic organizations should fund ten or more pilot colleges and universities that best propose to implement and demonstrate an exemplary teacher education program based on the criteria discussed in this book.

Recommendation: Public and private agencies that support development and innovation in science education for prospective teachers should build into their grant awards funding for adequate dissemination of the results of these efforts.

If science education for all children is to be improved, a national commitment to reforming preservice teacher education in science must be made. The reform must be concerted and comprehensive; it must result in the development and implementation of effective science education programs for prospective elementary school teachers and an active exchange of knowledge about reform activities and experiences. Only with a national commitment to such reform can the science learning of the nation's children begin to approach the lofty goals proclaimed by the president and the governors.

Current Practice in Science Education of Prospective Elementary School Teachers

Arie M. Michelsohn
Simon Hawkins

As an adjunct to our policy study of the preservice science education of prospective elementary school teachers, the National Center for Improving Science Education has collected information on this topic from 142 teacher education institutions across the country (see list at end of Appendix). The information was obtained largely through extensive telephone interviews with course instructors and program directors as well as through analyses of syllabi and other course materials. We used the information to develop a picture of current practice, identifying the various common approaches to teaching science content and science teaching methods to prospective elementary school teachers. We also attempted to identify programs and courses that represent particular innovations or that vary considerably from the norm.

Previous studies of preservice science programs (Mechling, Stedman, and Donnelan, 1982; Penick, 1987), present overviews of the requirements, structure, and philosophy of various programs. We found, however, that the *structure* of a program, the basis upon which different programs are usually compared, represents only one parameter for distinguishing one program from another. Two very different structures may actually be very similar to each other with respect to such other parameters as approach to and choice of activities for teaching science content and science pedagogy. Conversely, two very similar overall structures may differ a good deal in terms of other parameters. Our study therefore focused on actual activities, projects, assignments, and syllabi, along with questions about course and program goals and objectives, which we discussed with course faculty and program administrators. We found that, regardless of structure, philosophy, or particular program requirements, the means used for teaching science content and science pedagogy exhibit overlapping approaches that span a relatively small number of categories. These categories arise not from distinct differences in the different programs but from the particular ways in which the programs integrate their approaches to teaching content and pedagogy, to field experiences, to collaboration between faculty members and between institutions, and to the programs' overall structural organization.

Accordingly, we developed five different categories in which to classify individual programs:

1. Approach to teaching science content
2. Approach to teaching science pedagogy
3. Nature of field experiences that are part of pedagogy courses (as distinct from student teaching)
4. Extent or nature of collaboration between educators, scientists, and teachers
5. Overall structure of the program

A brief description of each of these categories and an overview of the subcategories (different approaches within each category) that we observed are given below.

Limitations

A few caveats are in order regarding our survey and this summary of it. First, our objective was to try to classify programs into as few categories as possible; hence, there is some overlap among categories and among subcategories. While we developed reasonably objective criteria for classifying programs, we occasionally had to make subjective decisions. Our full report (Michelsohn and Hawkins, forthcoming) contains profiles of individual programs that illustrate the variety of alternatives within each category and subcategory.

Second, our analysis is descriptive, not evaluative. Our purpose was primarily to categorize different approaches and configurations; no attempt was made to designate programs as "better" or "worse" relative to some standard.

Third, this summary of our survey serves as a general introduction to our process of categorizing programs and our findings on the distribution of program elements. Again, the full report provides more details.

Overview of the Analysis

This overview describes in general terms the distinguishing features of each category and subcategory and summarizes key findings.

1. Approach to teaching science content. Thirteen percent of the programs surveyed offer teacher education programs exclusively at the graduate level. These programs have no science content requirements; therefore, the science content categorization includes *undergraduate programs only*. We identified the following four approaches.

    a. *Standard undergraduate science courses.* The majority of teacher education programs in our study were undergraduate programs. These programs typically require teacher education students to take from one to four (usually two or three) science courses that are not specially designed for elementary education students. These courses often are the same ones that undergraduate nonscience majors take, although in some cases they are also introductory courses for majors. The majority of undergraduate elementary teacher education programs in our study, roughly two-thirds, set science requirements that are fulfilled through standard courses given in arts and sciences departments. In a few cases, we observed efforts to improve these introductory science courses through consultation with education faculty.

b. *Special courses using "transferrable" activities.* These courses are designed specifically for elementary education students and are oriented around activities, projects, and approaches used in such inquiry-based elementary school curricula as the *Elementary Science Study, Science Curriculum Improvement Study,* and *Science: A Process Approach.* Activities and projects often mentioned in such courses include "batteries and bulbs," "paper towels," and "camouflaged butterflies." These activities and projects sometimes serve as the basis for a discussion of content reoriented toward college-age students. Some of the content courses that fall into this category use middle school-type activities as well as activities more appropriate for lower grades. What distinguishes these courses from others is a core emphasis on using K–8 school activities as the basis for teaching science content to adults. Programs in this category appear to reflect the philosophy that the science content that prospective elementary school teachers should study ought to focus primarily on the subject matter they will be expected to teach. About a fifth of our total sample of programs fall into this category. This represents the overwhelming majority of science content courses specifically designed for teacher education students: of the one-third of institutions that offer such specially designed courses, about two-thirds use the transferrable-activities approach.

c. *Special courses using "nontransferrable" activities.* These courses are also designed specifically for elementary education students. Rather than being oriented toward elementary school science activities, they are more like traditional undergraduate science courses in terms of topic sequence and approach. Some of the courses in this category are oriented around themes (such as the environment); others take a more historical approach or concentrate on such processes as measurement and classification. While these courses may occasionally include modified elementary school activities (for example, "batteries and bulbs"), they strive to focus on phenomena and problems likely to be of more interest to adults than to children. Programs in this category appear to reflect the philosophy that prospective elementary school teachers need to learn science content in a manner that facilitates their developing general scientific literacy. Having a modicum of science understanding, it is believed, will provide these future teachers with a broad perspective from which they may draw as they teach particular subject matter to elementary school students. Six percent of all the programs in our sample fall into this category.

d. *Content and pedagogy courses combined.* In a small number (3 percent) of the programs in the sample, science content and methods are either both taught in the same course, or a parallel science methods seminar or recitation section is given in tandem with the science content courses. In cases where content and methods are taught within the same course, the focus is usually on "transferrable" activities. In cases where there is a parallel seminar or recitation, the content course is often a modified arts and sciences course, with the seminar or recitation serving as a bridge, if possible, between the content and associated activities and methods appropriate for elementary school students.

2. *Approach to teaching science pedagogy.* In this domain, we found that most of the programs surveyed also fall into four categories. (Three percent of the programs in our sample had no science pedagogy course requirements; 4 percent did not supply sufficient information to be classified.)

a. *Academic/pedagogical approach.* Methods courses in this category represent a small minority, 8 percent. They focus on such theoretical aspects of pedagogy as misconception research, constructivism, and learning theory and relate these ideas and concepts to practical science teaching situations. This approach treats pedagogy as an academic, research-oriented discipline that has distinct practical applications.

b. *Practical/pedagogical approach.* This category encompasses methods courses that focus on general pedagogical skills and concepts (for example, lesson planning, understanding child behavior and abilities, classroom management) as they apply to science teaching. This approach differs from the academic approach in that the assignments and content focus on teaching tasks rather than on research. Nearly half (48 percent) of the methods courses we examined fall into this category.

c. *Practical/science activities approach.* This category also encompasses methods courses that focus on pedagogical skills and concepts. The courses here, however, are organized around the performance of "transferrable" science activities, projects, and investigations that serve as a basis for discussion of pedagogical issues rather than around pedagogical themes for which selected science activities are undertaken as particular illustrations. Faculty who teach methods courses in this category are the most likely to consider as principal course objectives the development of science content knowledge, an understanding of the process of scientific inquiry, and/or the allaying of student fears about science. A third of the programs surveyed subscribe to this approach.

d. *Content and pedagogy courses combined.* See information in section 1(d) above.

3. Field experiences. All science methods courses provide some exposure to actual classroom science teaching distinct from the traditional student-teaching experience. The extent of the field experiences, the manner in which they are undertaken, and the role they play in the science methods courses vary. Our data indicate that three categories of field experiences are provided as part of science methods courses. (Twenty-seven percent of the programs in our total sample had no field requirements specific to science, and 4 percent did not supply sufficient information to be classified.)

a. *Standard model.* Methods courses in this category provide field experiences that encompass a range of activities: observing elementary science classrooms, interviewing individual elementary school students, teaching a small group of students, planning and teaching one lesson that is critiqued by peers. Typically, these field experiences total less than one-third of all course time; no *extended* field experience or practicum is specified as part of the science methods course. Elementary school teachers play a limited role in this model and usually do not undergo separate mentor teacher training in order to participate. Nearly two-thirds of the programs surveyed fall into this category.

b. *Professional development school (PDS) model.* The PDS model represents an institutional partnership in the education of future teachers, usually involving the close collaboration of master school teachers and postsecondary faculty. Field experiences in this model range from a relatively limited to a substantial portion of the science methods course. Since the PDS model is relatively young, the logistics and scope of integration of elementary schools with colleges, schools, and departments of education vary widely. There may not always be readily discernable differences between substantive field experiences in the "standard" model and those in a PDS model but—at least in concept—the PDS model is more conducive to substantive field experiences. Because of the growing popularity of the PDS concept, we grouped all institutions that subscribe to it in a distinct category, but they presently represent only 3 percent of the programs in our sample.

c. *Clinical model.* As the name implies, the clinical model stresses teacher education students working and studying in elementary schools beside classroom teachers. These field experiences typically constitute at least half the time allotted to science methods courses and generally make up most of the course. Seminars and discussion groups usually supplement the elementary classroom–based activities. The clinical model resembles an internship or apprenticeship Clinical programs tend to be more prevalent among fifth-year graduate programs; they appear to be increasing in popularity as states adopt policies that mandate "clinical master's" degrees as a prerequisite for teacher certification. Four percent of the programs in our study subscribe to the clinical model; this represents a fifth of the graduate programs.

4. Collaboration in program design and implementation. We identified three categories of collaboration. In general, all teacher education programs show some level of cooperation between education faculty and school teachers because student teaching requires it. In practice, such cooperation is sometimes tenuous. We looked for cases of real collaboration that extended well beyond cooperation or coordination. While the following categories may appear to construct a hierarchy, we did not pass judgment on the quality or efficacy of particular types of collaboration because more collaboration does not necessarily make for a better program. (Three percent of the programs in our study did not supply sufficient information to be classified in any of these categories.)

    a. *Vehicles for individual and institutional agreements.* This category is represented in nearly three-fourths of the programs and represents a basic level of cooperation between the arts and sciences and education faculties, on the one hand, and between postsecondary institutions and elementary schools on the other. Such cooperation has traditionally been necessary for the logistics of professional teacher education, in which professional course work is flanked by both general education in the liberal arts and clinical training in elementary schools. This basic-level cooperation remains the dominant arrangement in the field, although a number of the programs we surveyed that fall into this category have made concerted efforts to improve on traditional structures. Some of the types of collaboration within this category include teacher education students fulfilling their science content requirements through liberal arts courses, teacher education programs making logistical arrangements with elementary schools to accommodate student teaching, education faculty consulting with science faculty to improve undergraduate science teaching (in many cases such agreements extend to further collaboration), and school districts allowing selected teachers to assist with teaching methods courses as part of their assignments.

b. *Vehicles for joint planning.* Collaboration in this category usually involves some combination of education faculty, school teachers, and scientists meeting together, often as a committee or team, to plan a course or program. Individual *members* of the committees or teams may actually teach the planned course(s), but the committee as a whole mainly fulfills an oversight function. Sixteen percent of programs in our study subscribe to this subcategory of collaboration.

c. *Vehicles for joint implementation and research.* This category represents the greatest extent of collaboration, in which teams representing some combination of education faculty, school teachers, and scientists (sometimes along with other faculty from psychology, the social sciences, or other areas) not only plan courses but actually work together as a group with teacher education students on a day-to-day basis. A small percentage of institutions in our study (8 percent) conform to this category, and each has a particular interpretation of the nature of such collaboration.

5. Program structure. We also classified programs according to their overall structure. Most current institutional programs are at the undergraduate level and take four (sometimes five) years to complete. Over the past few years, the number of fifth-year graduate programs has increased considerably, often because of state mandates. These programs still represent the minority, however, even when alternative certification programs are included. While the number of fifth-year programs is likely to continue to increase, we found that their approaches to teaching science pedagogy are usually similar to those in current undergraduate programs. One difference, as noted above, is that graduate programs are much less likely to include science content requirements, although they may require demonstrated competence in science knowledge as a prerequisite for admission. In addition, fifth-year programs are more likely to be configured in an internship/apprenticeship structure than are

undergraduate programs. We have classified program structure into four broad categories. (Three percent of the programs in our study did not supply sufficient information to be classified in any of these categories.)

a.   *Standard.* This category represents program structures that follow the traditional sequence of general education followed by professional education (usually educational psychology, general and special methods, and so on) followed by student teaching. Included in this category are institutions that offer separately designated general and content-specific methods courses, such as social studies methods, reading methods, and science methods. Also included are institutions where mathematics and science methods are combined. Approximately 67 percent of the programs in our study have a standard structure.

b.   *Blocks.* This category is in some ways similar to the standard structure but differs in that all content-specific methods courses are blocked; that is, students take a single, multicredit course taught by several faculties rather than individual courses for fewer credits each. This appears to be a growing practice. The reasons for blocking content-specific methods vary from a need to reduce the total number of hours of education course work (sometimes occasioned by limitations set by the state) to a desire for real collaboration between various professions and integration of subject matter and approaches. Nearly 20 percent of the programs in our study subscribe to a block model.

c.   *Coordinated or structured.* Programs in this category closely coordinate subject matter courses, subject-specific methods courses, and student teaching experiences, and/or they designate a prescribed order in which preservice students must take a series of courses. About 10 percent of the programs in our study conform to this model.

d.   *Internship or Apprenticeship.* This category includes a small number of programs (3 percent of those included in our study) that take place almost entirely in schools. See section 3(c) above.

Cohorts

In addition to classifying institutions on the basis of the categories and subcategories described above, we found that a growing number of institutions are employing a *cohort* approach to teacher education. Cohort programs are those in which groups of students, ranging in size from a group of three or four to as many as thirty, fulfill program requirements together and often in a specified sequence.

A cohort is more than a particular class of students who are likely to take many courses together. Cohort members are encouraged to interact with one another on a regular basis, sharing intellectual insights and providing social and intellectual support. Small groups of faculty members occasionally work together as a cohort, and a faculty cohort may work with a student cohort. The use of cohorts is consistent in principle with many of the categories and subcategories we identified. Indeed, we observed the use of cohorts in a number of different types of programs. Nevertheless, fewer than 10 percent of the programs we studied utilize cohorts.

Institutions in Study

Allegheny College
Appalachian State University
Arizona State University
Arkansas State University-Main
  Campus
Auburn University-Main
  Campus
Ball State University
Bank Street College
Baylor University
Bloomsburg State University
Boston University
Bowling Green State
  University-Main Campus
Brigham Young University
Butler University
California State University at
  Chico
California State University at
  Dominguez Hills
California State University at
  Fullerton
California State University at
  Long Beach
California State University at
  San Bernardino
California State University at
  Stanislaus
California University of
  Pennsylvania
Capital College
Central Michigan University
Central Washington University
CUNY Brooklyn
CUNY City College
CUNY Hunter

Clarion University of
  Pennsylvania
Columbia University in the
  City of New York
Dakota State College
DePaul University
East Carolina University
East Tennessee State University
Eastern Illinois University
Eastern Michigan University
Eastern New Mexico
  University-Main Campus
Emporia State University
Florida International
  University
Florida State University
Glassboro State College
Grand Valley State University
Hampton University
Harvard University
Hope College
Illinois State University
Indiana State University
Indiana University at
  Bloomington
Indiana University of
  Pennsylvania
Indiana University-Purdue at
  Fort Wayne
Iowa State University
Jacksonville State University
James Madison University
Kansas State University of Agri-
  culture and Applied Science
Kean College of New Jersey
Kearney State College

Kent State University-Main Campus
Kutztown University of Pennsylvania
Lamar University
Long Island University-C.W. Post Campus
Madonna College
Mankato State University
Memphis State University
Miami University at Oxford
Michigan State University
Millersville University of Pennsylvania
Mississippi State University
Morehead State University
North Carolina Central University
Northern Illinois University
Nova University
Ohio State University-Main Campus
Ohio University-Main Campus
Old Dominion University
Pennsylvania State University-Main Campus
Purdue University-Main Campus
Radford University
St. Cloud State University
Sam Houston State University
San Diego State University
San Francisco State University
San Jose State University
Southern Arkansas University-Main Campus
Southern Illinois State University at Edwardsville

Southern Oregon State College
Springfield College
SUNY College at Buffalo
SUNY College at Fredonia
SUNY College at Oneonta
Stephen F. Austin State University
Syracuse University-Main Campus
Texas A & M University
Texas Tech University
Texas Women's College
Towson State University
University of Akron-Main Campus
University of Alabama at Birmingham
University of Alabama at Huntsville
University of Alabama at Tuscaloosa
University of California at Berkeley
University of Central Florida
University of Dayton
University of Delaware
University of Georgia
University of Houston at Clear Lake
University of Illinois at Urbana
University of Iowa
University of Maine at Farmington
University of Maryland at College Park
University of Massachusetts at Amherst

University of Michigan at Ann
Arbor
University of Minnesota at
Twin Cities
University of Missouri at
Columbia
University of Nebraska at
Lincoln
University of Nevada at Reno
University of New Mexico–
Main Campus
University of New Orleans
University of North Carolina at
Charlotte
University of North Carolina at
Wilmington
University of North Texas
University of Northern
Colorado
University of Northern Iowa
University of South Florida
University of Southern Maine
University of Southern
Mississippi
University of Tennessee at
Knoxville

University of Texas at Austin
University of Toledo
University of Utah
University of Wisconsin at
Madison
University of Wisconsin at
Milwaukee
University of Wisconsin at
Oshkosh
University of Wisconsin at
White Water
University of Wyoming
Vanderbilt University
Washington State University at
Pullman
Weber State University
West Chester University of
Pennsylvania
West Virginia State University
West Virginia University
Western Kentucky State
University
Western Washington University
Wichita State University
Winthrop College

References

Alexander, R. M. *Animal Mechanics*. (2nd ed.). Oxford, England: Blackwell Scientific Publications, 1983.

Alexander, R. M. *Dynamics of Dinosaurs and Other Extinct Giants*. New York: Columbia University Press, 1989.

American Association for the Advancement of Science. *Project 2061: Science for All Americans*. Washington, D.C.: American Association for the Advancement of Science, 1989.

American Association for the Advancement of Science. *The Liberal Art of Science: Agenda for Action*. Washington D.C.: Project on Liberal Education and the Sciences, American Association for the Advancement of Science, 1990.

American Association of Colleges for Teacher Education. *Research About Teacher Education III, Teaching Teachers: Facts and Figures*. Washington, D.C.: Research About Teacher Education Project, American Association of Colleges for Teacher Education, 1989.

American Association of University Women. *How Schools Shortchange Girls*. Washington, D.C.: American Association of University Women, 1992.

American Psychological Association. *Learner-Centered Psychological Principles: Guidelines for School Redesign and Reform*. Washington, D.C.: American Psychological Association, 1991.

Arons, A. "Achieving Wider Scientific Literacy." *Daedalus,* Spring 1983, pp. 91–122.

Atkin, J. M. "Teaching as Research." Paper presented at the annual meeting of the American Educational Research Association, Chicago, Apr. 1991.

Baird, J. R., Fensham, P. J., Gunstone, R. F., and White, R. T. "The Importance of Reflection in Improving Science Teaching and Learning." *Journal of Research in Science Teaching,* 1991, *28*(2), 163–182.

Barrow, L. H. "Professional Preparation and Responsibilities of New England Preservice Elementary Science Methods Faculty." *Science Education,* 1987, *71*(4), 557–564.

Berliner, D. C. "In Pursuit of the Expert Pedagogue." *Educational Researcher,* Aug./Sept. 1986, pp. 5–13.

Black, A., and Ammon, P. "A Developmental-Constructivist Approach to Teacher Education." *Journal of Teacher Education,* 1992, *43*(5), 323–335.

Black, P. J. "The School Science Curriculum: Principles for a Framework." In A. B. Champagne and L. E. Hornig (eds.), *The Science Curriculum: This Year in School Science 1986.* Washington, D.C., American Association for the Advancement of Science, 1987.

Blank, R. K., and Dalkilic, M. *State Policies on Science and Mathematics Education, 1992.* Washington, D.C.: State Education Assessment Center, Council of Chief State School Officers, 1992.

Boyer, E. *College: The Undergraduate Experience in America.* New York: Harper & Row, 1987.

Brousseau, B., and Freeman, D. *Entering Teacher Candidate Interviews—Fall 1982. Research and Evaluation in Teacher Education.* OPE Technical Report No. 5. East Lansing: Michigan State University, 1984.

Bybee, R. W., and others. *Science and Technology Education for the Elementary Years: Frameworks for Curriculum and Instruction.* Andover, Mass.: National Center for Improving Science Education, The NETWORK, Inc., 1989.

Calderhead, J. "The Role of Reflection in Learning to Teach." In L. Valli (ed.), *Reflective Teacher Education.* Albany, N.Y.: State University of New York Press, 1992.

Carnegie Forum on Education and the Economy. *A Nation Prepared: Teachers for the 21st Century.* Washington, D.C.: Task

Force on Teaching as a Profession, Carnegie Forum on Education and the Economy, 1986.

Clark, C. M. "Research on Teaching and the Content of Teacher Education Programs: An Optimistic View." Paper presented at the annual meeting of the American Educational Research Association, New Orleans, Apr. 1984.

Clewell, B. C., Anderson, T. A., and Thorpe, M. E. *Breaking the Barriers: Helping Female and Minority Students Succeed in Mathematics and Science.* San Francisco: Jossey-Bass, 1992.

Clifford, J. W., and Guthrie, G. J. *Ed School.* Chicago: University of Chicago Press, 1988.

Cochran, K. F., King, R. A., and DeRuiter, J. A. "Pedagogical Content Knowing: An Integrative Model for Teacher Preparation." *Journal of Teacher Education,* in press.

Colton, A. B., and Sparks-Langer, G. "A Conceptual Framework to Guide the Development of Teacher Reflection and Decision Making." *Journal of Teacher Education,* 1993, *44*(1), 45–54.

Conant, J. B. *The Education of American Teachers.* New York: McGraw-Hill, 1963.

Cronin-Jones, L. L. "Science Teacher Beliefs and Their Influence on Curriculum Implementation: Two Case Studies." *Journal of Research in Science Teaching,* 1991, *28*(3), 235–250.

Cross, P. "The Adventures of Education in Wonderland: Implementing Education Reform." *Phi Delta Kappan,* 1987, *68*(7), 496–502.

Crow, N. A. "Preservice Teachers' Biography: A Case Study." Paper presented at the annual meeting of the American Educational Research Association, Washington, D.C., Apr. 1987.

Dana, T. M., and Parsons, S. "Preservice Teachers' Biography: A Case Study." Paper presented at the annual meeting of the American Educational Research Association, Washington, D.C., Apr. 1991.

Darwin, C. *The Structure and Distribution of Coral Reefs.* London: Smith, Elder, 1842.

Darwin, C. *The Formation of Vegetable Mould, Through the Action of Worms, with Observations on Their Habits.* London: John Murray, 1881.

Driver, R., Guesne, E., and Tiberghien, A. (eds.). *Children's Ideas in Science.* Philadelphia: Open University Press, 1985.

Federal Coordinating Council for Science, Engineering, and Technology. *By the Year 2000: First in the World.* Washington, D.C.: Committee on Education and Human Resources, Federal Coordinating Council for Science, Engineering, and Technology (c/o National Aeronautics and Space Administration), 1991.

Federal Coordinating Council for Science, Engineering, and Technology. *Pathways to Excellence: A Federal Strategy for Science, Mathematics, Engineering, and Technology Education.* Washington, D.C.: Committee on Education and Human Resources, Federal Coordinating Council for Science, Engineering, and Technology (c/o National Aeronautics and Space Administration), 1993.

Feiman-Nemser, S., McDiarmid, G. W., Melnick, S., and Parker, M. *Changing Beginning Teachers' Conceptions: A Study of an Introductory Teacher Education Course."* East Lansing: National Center for Research on Teacher Education and Department of Teacher Education, Michigan State University, 1988.

Ford, D. C., and Varney, H. L. "How Students See Scientists: Mostly Male, Mostly White, and Mostly Benevolent." *Science and Children,* 1989, *26*(8), 8–13.

Fosnot, C. T. *Enquiring Teachers, Enquiring Learners: A Constructivist Approach for Teaching.* New York: Teachers College Press, 1989.

Gardner, A. L., Cochran, K. F., and Tobin, K. G. *Critical Issues in Reforming Elementary Teacher Preparation in Mathematics and Science: Conference Proceedings.* Greeley: University of Northern Colorado, 1993.

Gardner, H. *Frames of Mind.* New York: Basic Books, 1983.

Goodlad, J. I. "Studying the Education of Educators: From Conception to Findings." *Phi Delta Kappan,* 1990, *71*(9), 698–701.

Goodlad, J. I. *Teachers for Our Nation's Schools.* San Francisco: Jossey-Bass, 1991.

Gould, S. J. "Evolution and the Triumph of Homology, or Why History Matters." *American Scientist,* 1986, *74*, 60–69.

Grayson, D. A., and Martin, M. D. *Gender/Ethnic Expectations and*

Student Achievement. Earlham, Iowa: GrayMill Foundation, 1988.

Guild, P. B., and Garger, S. *Marching to Different Drummers.* Alexandria, Va.: Association for Supervision and Curriculum Development, 1985.

Harrington, H. L., and Garrison, J. W. "Cases as Shared Inquiry: A Dialogical Model of Teacher Preparation." *American Educational Research Journal,* 1992, *29*(4), 715–735.

Hodgkinson, H. *All One System: Demographics of Education, Kindergarten Through Graduate School.* Washington, D.C.: Institute for Educational Leadership, 1985.

Hoffman, N. *Woman's True Profession: Voices from the History of Teaching.* New York: McGraw-Hill, 1981.

Holmes Group. *Tomorrow's Teachers.* East Lansing, Mich.: Holmes Group, 1986.

Huling-Austin, L., and Murphy, S. C. "Assessing the Impact of Teacher Induction Programs: Implications for Program Development." Paper presented at the annual meeting of the American Educational Research Association, Washington, D.C., Apr. 1987.

International Association for the Evaluation of Educational Achievement. *Science Achievement in Seventeen Countries: A Preliminary Report.* Elmsford, N.Y.: Pergamon Press, 1988.

Jasalavich, S. M. "Preservice Elementary Teachers' Beliefs About Science Teaching and Learning and Perceived Sources of Their Beliefs Prior to Their First Formal Science Teaching Experience." Paper presented at the annual meeting of the National Association for Research in Science Teaching, Boston, Mar. 1992.

Johnson, D. W., Johnson, R. T., Holubec, E. J., and Roy, P. *Circles of Learning: Cooperation in the Classroom.* Alexandria, Va.: Association for Supervision and Curriculum Development, 1984.

Johnston, J. M., and Kay, R. "The Role of Institutions of Higher Education in Professional Teacher Induction." In D. M. Brooks (ed.), *Teacher Induction: A New Beginning.* Reston, Va.: Association of Teacher Educators, 1987.

Jones, L. R., and others. *The 1990 Science Report Card: NAEP's Assessment of Fourth, Eighth, and Twelfth Graders.* Washington, D.C.: National Center for Education Statistics, 1992.

Kerman, S. "Teacher Expectations and Student Achievement." *Phi Delta Kappan,* 1979, *60*(10), 716–718.

Kidder, T. *Among Schoolchildren.* Boston: Houghton Mifflin, 1989.

Kirby, S. N., and Hudson, S. "Black Teachers in Indiana: A Potential Shortage?" *Educational Evaluation and Policy Analysis,* 1993, *15*(2), 181–194.

Kolb, D. A. *Experimental Learning: Experience as the Source of Learning and Development.* Englewood Cliffs, N.J.: Prentice-Hall, 1984.

Koretz, D., and others. *The Reliability of Scores from the 1992 Vermont Portfolio Assessment Program: Interim Report.* Washington, D.C.: National Center for Research on Evaluation, Standards, and Student Testing, RAND Corporation, 1992.

Krajcik, J. S., and others. "Integrating Knowledge Bases: An Upper-Elementary Teacher Preparation Program Emphasizing the Teaching of Science." In P. Rubba, L. Campbell, and T. Danna (eds.), *Educating Teachers of Science.* Columbus, Ohio: ERIC Clearinghouse for Science, Mathematics, and Environmental Education, 1993.

Kyle, W. C. "The Reform Agenda and Science Education: Hegemonic Control vs. Counterhegemony." *Science Education,* 1991, *75*(4), 403–411.

Lampert, M., and Ball, D. L. *Using Hypermedia Technology to Support a New Pedagogy of Teacher Education.* Issue Paper 90-5. East Lansing: National Center for Research on Teacher Education, Michigan State University, 1990.

Lapointe, A. E., Askew, J. M., and Mead, N. A. *Learning Science.* Princeton, N.J.: Educational Testing Service, 1992.

Little, J. W. "Norms of Collegiality and Experimentation: Workplace Conditions of School Success. *American Educational Research Journal,* 1982, *19*(3), 325-340.

Loucks-Horsley, S., and others. *Developing and Supporting Teachers for Elementary School Science Education.* Andover, Mass.: National Center for Improving Science Education, The NETWORK, Inc., 1989.

Mastain, R. *The NASDTEC Manual: Manual on Certification and Preparation of Educational Personnel in the United States.* Sacramento, Calif.: National Association of State Directors of Teacher Education and Certification, 1991.

Mechling, K. R., Stedman, C. H., and Donnelan, K. M. "An NSTA Report: Preparing and Certifying Science Teachers." *Science and Children*, Oct. 1982, pp. 9–14.

Michelsohn, A. M., and Hawkins, S. "An Anecdotal Study of Current Practice in the Preservice Science Education of Elementary School Teachers: Preliminary Analysis." Paper presented at the annual meeting of the Association for the Education of Teachers in Science, Charleston, S.C., Jan. 30, 1993.

Michelsohn, A. M., and Hawkins, S. *A Qualitative Study of Preservice Elementary Teacher Preparation Programs in Science.* Andover, Mass.: National Center for Improving Science Education, The NETWORK, Inc., forthcoming.

National Board for Professional Teaching Standards. *Toward High and Rigorous Standards for the Teaching Profession: Initial Policies and Perspectives of the National Board for Professional Teaching Standards.* Detroit, Mich.: National Board for Professional Teaching Standards, 1991.

National Board for Professional Teaching Standards. *1991 Annual Report.* Detroit, Mich.: National Board for Professional Teaching Standards, 1992.

National Center for Improving Science Education. *Getting Started in Science: A Blueprint for Elementary School Science Education.* Andover, Mass.: National Center for Improving Science Education, 1989.

National Council for Accreditation of Teacher Education. *Conditions & Procedures for STATE/NCATE Partnerships.* Washington, D.C.: National Council for Accreditation of Teacher Education, 1993.

National Education Association. *Status of the American Public School Teacher: 1990–1991.* Washington, D.C.: National Education Association, 1992.

National Education Goals Panel. *The National Education Goals Report: Building a Nation of Learners.* Washington, D.C.: National Education Goals Panel, 1991.

National Science Board. *Science & Engineering Indicators—1989.* Washington, D.C.: U.S. Government Printing Office, 1989.

National Science Teachers Association. *NSTA Standards for Science Teacher Preparation*. Washington, D.C.: National Science Teachers Association, 1983.

National Science Teachers Association. *NSTA Standards for Science Teacher Preparation*. Washington, D.C.: National Science Teachers Association, 1992.

Northwest Equals Program. *Family Science*. Portland, Oreg.: Portland State University, in press.

Oakes, J. "Grouping Students for Instruction." In M. C. Alkin (ed.), *Encyclopedia of Educational Research*. Vol. 2. New York: Macmillan, 1982.

Oakes, J. *Lost Talent: The Underparticipation of Women, Minorities, and Disabled Persons in Science*. Santa Monica, Calif.: RAND Corporation, 1990.

Osborne, M. "Teaching With and Without Mirrors: Examining Science Teaching from the Perspective of a Teacher and a Learner." Unpublished doctoral dissertation, Michigan State University, 1993.

Pearson, W., Jr. *Black Scientists, White Society, and Colorless Science: A Study of Universalism in American Science*. Millwood, N.Y.: Associated Faculty Press, 1985.

Penick, J. (ed.). *Focus on Excellence: Preservice Elementary Teacher Education in Science*. Report vol. 4, no. 3. Washington, D.C.: National Science Teachers Association, 1987.

Prather, J. P. "Philosophical Examination of the Problem of the Unlearning of Incorrect Science Concepts." Paper presented at the annual meeting of the National Association for Research in Science Teaching, French Lick Springs, Ind.: Apr. 1985.

Project 30 Alliance. *Project 30 Year Two Report: Institutional Accomplishments*. Newark: University of Delaware, 1991.

Raizen, S. A. "The Reform of Science Education in the U.S.A.: Déjà Vu or De Novo?" *Studies in Science Education*, 1991, *19*, 1–41.

Raizen, S. A., and Britton, T. "Science and Mathematics Teachers." In National Science Foundation, *Indicators of Science and Mathematics Education*, Washington, D.C.: National Science Foundation, 1993.

Raizen, S. A., and others. *Assessment in Elementary School Science*

Education. Andover, Mass.: National Center for Improving Science Education, The NETWORK, Inc., 1989.

Reynolds, A. "What Is Competent Beginning Teaching? A Review of the Literature." *Review of Educational Research,* 1992, *62*(1), 1–35.

Risner, G. P., Skeel, D. J., and Nicholson, J. I. "A Closer Look at Textbooks." *Science and Children,* 1992, *30*(1), 42–45, 73.

Roth, K. J. "Science Education: It's Not Enough to 'Do' or 'Relate.'" *American Educator,* Winter 1989, pp. 16–22, 46–48.

Roth, K. J., and others. "Teacher and Researcher Development in a Professional Development School: Learning About Elementary Science Teaching from Multiple Perspectives." Paper presented at the annual meeting of the National Association for Research in Science Teaching, Boston, 1992.

Schön, D. A. *Educating the Reflective Practitioner: Toward a New Design for Teaching and Learning in the Professions.* San Francisco: Jossey-Bass, 1987.

Shavelson, R. J., and others. "Performance Assessment in Science." *Applied Measurement in Education,* 1991, *4*(4), 347–362.

Shulman, L. S. "Knowledge and Teaching: Foundations of the New Reform." In M. Okazawa-Rey, J. Anderson, and R. Traver (eds.), *Teachers, Teaching, & Teacher Education.* Cambridge, Mass.: Harvard Educational Review, 1987.

Shymansky, J. "Using Constructivist Ideas to Teach Science Teachers Constructivism, or Teachers Are Students." *Journal of Science Teacher Education,* 1992, *3*(2), 53–57.

Silverman, R., and Welty, W. *Case Studies for Teacher Problem Solving.* New York: McGraw-Hill, 1992.

Sparks, G., and Simmons, S. "Inquiry Oriented Staff Development: Using Research as a Source of Tools Not Rules." In S. D. Caldwell, *Staff Development: A Handbook of Effective Practices.* Oxford, Ohio: National Staff Development Council, 1988.

Spencer, G. *Projections of the Population of the United States, by Age, Sex, and Race: 1988 to 2080.* U.S. Bureau of the Census. Current Population Reports: Population Estimates and Projects (Series P-25, No. 1018). Washington, D.C.: U.S. Government Printing Office, 1989.

Thomas, K., and Olson, E. C. (eds.). *A Cold Look at the Warm-*

Blooded Dinosaurs: Selected Symposia Series. Boulder, Colo.: American Association for the Advancement of Science, 1980.

Tobias, S. *Revitalizing Undergraduate Science: Why Some Things Work and Most Don't.* Tucson, Ariz.: Research Corporation, 1992.

Tyson, H. *Who Will Teach the Children? Progress and Resistance in Teacher Education.* San Francisco: Jossey-Bass, 1994.

U.S. Department of Education, Office of Educational Research and Improvement. *Youth Indicators: Trends in the Well-Being of American Youth.* Washington, D.C.: U.S. Government Printing Office, 1988.

U.S. Department of Education, National Center for Educational Statistics. *Schools and Staffing in the United States: A Statistical Profile, 1987–1988.* Washington, D.C.: U.S. Government Printing Office, 1992a.

U.S. Department of Education, National Center for Educational Statistics. *Digest of Education Statistics: 1992.* Washington, D.C.: U.S. Government Printing Office, 1992b.

U.S. Department of Education, National Center for Educational Statistics. *The Condition of Education.* Washington, D.C.: U.S. Government Printing Office, 1992c.

U.S. Department of Education, National Center for Educational Statistics. *Projections of Education Statistics to 2001: An Update.* Washington, D.C.: U.S. Government Printing Office, 1993a.

U.S. Department of Education, Office of Educational Research and Improvement. *New Teachers in the Job Market, 1991 Update.* Washington, D.C.: U.S. Government Printing Office, 1993b.

Van Maanen, M. "Linking Ways of Knowing with Ways of Being Practical." *Curriculum Inquiry,* 1977, *6,* 205–228.

Visser, M. *Much Depends on Dinner: The Extraordinary History and Mythology, Allure and Obsessions, Perils and Taboos of an Ordinary Meal.* Toronto: McClelland and Stewart, 1986.

Vitale, M. R., and Romance, N. R. "Using Videodisk Instruction in an Elementary Science Methods Course: Remediating Science Knowledge Deficiencies and Facilitating Science Teaching Attitudes." *Journal of Research in Science Teaching,* 1992, *29*(9), 915–928.

Vygotsky, L. *Thought and Language.* Cambridge, Mass.: Harvard University Press, 1986.

Watson, B., and Konicek, R. "Teaching for Conceptual Change: Confronting Children's Experience." *Phi Delta Kappan,* 1990, *71*(9), 680–685.

Weinstein, C. S. "Teacher Education Students' Preconceptions of Teaching." *Journal of Teacher Education,* 1989, *40,* 53–60.

Weinstein, C. S. "Prospective Elementary Teachers' Beliefs About Teaching: Implications for Teacher Education." *Teaching and Teacher Education,* 1990, *6,* 279–290.

Weiss, I. R. *Report of the 1985–86 National Survey of Science and Mathematics Education.* Research Triangle Park, N.C.: Research Triangle Institute, 1987.

Wong, M. J., and Osguthorpe, R. T. "The Continuing Domination of the Four-Year Teacher Education Program: A National Survey." *Journal of Teacher Education,* 1993, *44*(1), 64–70.

Yager, R. E., and Penick, J. E. "Science Teacher Education." In W. R. Houston (ed.), *Handbook of Research on Teacher Education.* New York: Macmillan, 1990.

Yager, R. E., and Zehr, E. "Science Education in US Graduate Institutions During Two Decades." *Science Education,* 1985, *69*(2), 163–169.

Young, B. J., and Kellogg, T. "Science Attitudes and Preparation of Preservice Elementary Teachers." In Duschl, R. (ed.), *Science Education,* June 1993, *77*(3), 279–291.

Index